THE
$100,000,000
MARCH

How to Enjoy the Lifestyle of Your Dreams
Instead of Just Making Other People Rich

ALLEN KRONEBUSCH

The $100,000,000 March: How to Enjoy the Lifestyle of Your
Dreams Instead of Just Making Other People Rich
Copyright 2008 by DEDFIL Productions, LLC

First Printing, June 2008
ISBN 978-0-9817830-2-4

Book design and layout by Sadie Cross
Printed in the United States of America

This book is dedicated to my sons Ethan and Aiden.

May this book serve as an *example to follow* –

Persevere,
be bold,
and always keep your word.

ACKNOWLEDGEMENTS

While writing this book, I spent a great deal of time reflecting upon the people who and circumstances that most affected my personal growth. This is my opportunity to say "Thank You" specifically to those who have helped me to enjoy the lifestyle of my childhood dreams.

To my wife, Debbie: You are my best friend both in and out of the office, my most trusted ally. You have always believed in me, sometimes more than I believed in myself – you are my rock.

To my sons: Even though you are too young to understand, you have inspired me to be better. Because of you, I now see the world in a different light, and have opened my mind and heart in ways I never conceived.

To my dad and stepmother: You shaped me in so many ways that ultimately helped develop my inner strength. You both remained steadfast, a trait I have constantly mirrored. Dad, you have been my example of what it means to be a man.

To Sandy: You believed in a 19-year old kid enough to go out on a limb, and continued encouraging me over the years.

To my grandmother, Donna: You always believed in and supported me.

To my friends, mentors, and APO brothers, Russ Glover, Brian Mihm, Brad Bunker, Joe Repice, Steve Libera, Fran Yahnke, Dennis Lamkin, and Zoltan Zenda: You helped me when I needed it most.

To my earliest customers: Knowingly or not, you assisted a young man to build his confidence and skills, spawning an ever-growing empire.

To my entire Kronebusch family, especially my grandparents, Gerald and Theresa, uncles Andy and Dale, and brother Jason: Thank you for building such a good reputation, thereby opening many doors and providing me my early start.

To the thousands of both examples-to-follow and warning-signs-of-what-not-to-do encountered on my lifestyle journey: I have learned much from both of you.

To Paul Gaspord, Deb Evans, Greg Pinneo, Jim Rohn, Mark Ostrofsky, Roxanne Harris and William Bailey: You are special people who have assisted significantly in one or more of my business ventures.

To my fellow EO Empire Builders: Thank you for your inspiration and dedication to our group's vision.

TABLE OF CONTENTS

STEP 2
Where Are You Now?   57

Truth # 6   *The higher your Life GPA,*
                         the more enjoyable your lifestyle.   113

STEP 3
Where Are You Going?   161

Truth # 7   *Success in life is a journey,*
                 NOT a destination.   163

Truth # 8   *Never ever quit!*   179

Truth # 9   *Learning to fish will set you free!*   193

Bonus

FOREWORD

My name is William Bailey and I'm 77 years old. With the exception of the first 25 years of my life, my entire career has been in sales and marketing. It has been my good fortune to participate in creating or founding three major corporations. During that time, I became very familiar with people who became famous in the field of personal development, even more concentrated in the fields of marketing and sales training.

I asked Allen Kronebusch if he would permit me to write a forward to the book you are now about to read. Mr. Kronebusch is uniquely qualified to write a book about sales, sales training and leadership, a possible career in sales, as well as personal development, because he has lived what he is writing. I saw Allen start as a very young man with no training in the difficult world of direct sales. Since that time, he has formed multiple companies, one of which markets safety equipment directly to residences and industries around the world.

Unlike the many books on sales and selling, which have been written by people who primarily get degrees in communications, and base their books on interviews of other people involved in sales, this is a book that Allen Kronebusch has *lived*. His suggestions of how to think and how to sell have real value and reward that only a career in sales and leadership can bring. His more than 18 years of actual experience of not only selling, but teaching hundreds and even thousands of other people how to earn unusual incomes as a result of selling, is what THIS book is based upon.

I recommend this book completely and totally because it is real information written by a person with real experience and written in such a manner that anyone can use this information for their own personal growth.

PREFACE

Nothing is so powerful
as an idea whose time has come!
-- Victor Hugo

I have asked literally thousands of people whether they were winners or losers and, as to be expected, almost all of them unequivocally stated they were winners. Then the moment of truth arrived, in which they had the opportunity to back up their words with actions, and most failed to break free from "loser" status and become everlasting winners.

I may seem harsh or overly blunt but I believe you did not start reading this book because you were searching for more fluff or hype. The world I see has become so full of "feel-good" messages that fail to emphasize that all true "good" feelings come from inside. We all know deep down whether we are winners or losers. We know how we respond when challenged. We know whether we find a way to succeed or just another excuse to justify our current position so the sting of yet another defeat does not feel so bad. No matter how many times the outside world may tell us to feel good just because we exist, those of us who are bona fide winners inherently know the only way to be a winner is to WIN at the most important game of all, the game of life.

One beautiful spring day, my life coach and I were driving through the hills of Kentucky. He was showing me the hollow where he grew up. I did my best to imagine what his childhood was like with no running water, no electricity, and 11 children living in a house the size of my living room. I thought that if anyone truly understood the difference between winners and losers, it must be William Bailey, a very successful businessman. So I said, "You started with nothing but achieved so much. You have worked with millions of people directly and indirectly over the last 50 years to help them do the same. What have you learned is the real difference between winners and losers?" He thought about it for a moment and then told me this:

Each of us has been given our own set of challenging circumstances. We are obligated to overcome these in order to live the life we desire. The true difference between winners and losers is how much of their past they allow to affect their future.

He went on to say:

☺ *Winners have an innate sense of when something is wrong and they search for ways to make it right.*

☺ *Winners are unhappy with the status quo and are willing to do something about it.*

☹ *Losers allow the past to overwhelm them, often to the point that they become proud of their cynicism and are bitter, nasty and negative.*

☹ *Losers are unwilling to change or grow and have given up, accepted their fate and are no longer willing to fight.*

He concluded with:

Becoming a winner is a process of prying loose from what holds you back. For this process, people need an atmosphere that is overwhelmingly more influential than what has happened to them in the past. People grow or die on the same course unless they are met by a stronger opposing force that inspires them to change. All positions in life are temporary and the river of time does not flow in reverse for anyone. Every day is an opportunity for personal growth. Just because someone has been a loser in the past has NO bearing on the future, unless they permit it to.

Winners are winners because they make a conscious choice to be winners by focusing every ounce of their daily effort on winning and settling for nothing less.

I have a vision ...

I call it **The $100,000,000 March™**. I believe there are winners out there currently living the lives of losers only because they have never been affected by a force strong enough to wake them up to what life could be for them. **The $100,000,000 March™** is a movement, a powerful idea whose time has come!

The $100,000,000 March™ started as my personal vision of a human development movement that will yield in excess of $100,000,000 in annual revenues based upon teaching people how to be winners. Now the vision is becoming like a wildfire of excitement. Much like the snowball gaining momentum as it rolls down the mountain only to become an avalanche, nothing is more powerful than helping another person reach his or her true potential. This book along with our team and its tools will make this vision a reality.

How?

Step 1

Develop 100 case studies of people who earned at least $8,333 in a month after applying the information learned from this book – *100 Earning $100,000*™ (www.100E100.com).

Step 2

Analyze the case studies to create educational tools and accountability systems to market to the world.

Step 3

Generate $100,000,000 in gross sales of our coaching products which help those willing to do whatever is necessary to enjoy the lifestyles of their dreams.

Within these pages is your beginning: Three Steps to earn your first $100,000 within this next year. Each Step is broken down further into Three Truths to fully explain the step. One Vision + Three Steps + Nine Truths = a life-changing opportunity for every average American to rise up and prove to the world how above-average he or she really is.

Welcome to the team!

Now it is time to get to work because we all have much to do!

- Allen Kronebusch

Existing on autopilot will only keep you stationary. When we forget where we started from, we are destined to return to that place. Therefore, every person who wants an extraordinary lifestyle must use the information taught in the next three Truths to improve their awareness of where they have been and understanding of WHY they were there so they can pry loose from what holds them back.

Learn from your past in order to benefit your present and future.

Absence of an option
makes the mind grow stronger.

I had no other option ...

TRUTH # 1

Decide what YOUR lifestyle will be, or someone else will!

I was adopted at age 6 and grew up in Winona, Minnesota, a small Midwestern city of 25,000. I was part of the first generation not to grow up on a farm, was the oldest child, and by far the oldest of more than 40 grandchildren.

When I was 9 years old, my dad got custody of me from the last foster home I lived in. It started rough but my dad hung tough. Until my dad got on his feet after he and my mother divorced, my 2-year old brother, dad, and I slept on a single mattress on the living room floor. As part of the divorce settlement, my dad just wanted the house so he could raise us boys and my mother took everything else. As a family we had nothing except each other.

My dad was high-school educated and worked for the railroad as a laborer. He was never sick, nor late, and always set a strong example of working hard for what you get. I can remember many mornings when my brother and I stayed in our warm bed and our dad had to get up to clean ice off the train track switches. It was freezing cold and pitch black at 4 a.m., but he still went and I never remember him complaining about it. Just like the life he led, my father was very strong, disciplined, black-and-white, and that is how he raised his sons. It was not an easy time for any of us but, oh the lessons I learned …

1.1   Make a Decision

I believe that a decision is the BIG picture objective and commitments are numerous steps made along the journey to seeing your decision become real. When I was about 10 in 1980 I saw something on television that said going through life is like driving a car – you can either be in the driver's seat or in the passenger's seat. As the driver, you're in control. You don't get the opportunity to enjoy the scenery as much as the passenger does, but wherever the driver wants to go, the passenger must follow. Being in the driver's seat metaphorically is the same as owning your own business, and being in the passenger's seat is like working for someone else. That really stuck with me, and I realized that there are pluses and minuses to whichever seat you choose.

Both the driver (owner) and passenger (employee) take risks, but the driver has the greatest potential gains in freedom and financial rewards. I made a decision early on that I needed to be in the driver's seat, an entrepreneur. I wanted to be a successful business person and own my own business. I saw what having a J.O.B. (Just Over Broke) was doing to my dad, how he traded his health for a paycheck. I saw that when the employer does not need you any longer, they simply lay you off. In a small town when the employer calls you to come back, everybody I saw came running. The employee thinks they have "job security" – that is what I constantly heard growing up. However, since when is security defined as prolonged poverty? The government won't allow you to starve and I know this because I too ate the handouts of powdered milk and government cheese, therefore I thought at a young age that actual security would only come from inside ME. I decided that no matter the risk, I had to take control of my life and be the driver or I would continue to be pushed around by the employer and treated like a puppet on a string. I did not want some boss to tell me when I could vacation with my family or if I could have the time to see my child play baseball. I did not want to have to ask permission to use the restroom or tell me what renting my time to them was worth. I decided to be free and was willing to pay the price, no matter what it took, at the ripe old age of 10. What choice did I have? I love, respect, and appreciate my dad very much but absolutely knew his life of working hard for little money was not for me.

I did not know how I was going to get there, but I DECIDED to make the journey. That was the single most critical step for me, because when I made that decision I also made a commitment to myself that no matter what it took I would keep on moving toward my desired lifestyle. I yearned to be free. Many times since I made this decision, life seemed all uphill and I felt alone in my quest, but I refused to give in no matter how tough it became. The personal strength I gained by this mindset cannot be overstated. Over and over I found a way to beat the challenges life threw at me which, in turn, made me more confident and capable of facing even greater obstacles later in life. Life is not a dress-rehearsal. This is the real deal. If you do not decide what you need your life to be and commit to achieving that vision no matter what it takes, someone else will decide for you and you may not be happy with what they chose.

1.2 Turn challenge into achievement

It was late fall of 1982 and my dad said to me, "Son, you are old enough now to start taking care of yourself. From now on, you will pay for your own school lunch and anything else you want that is extra." I was 12, in 7th grade at the time, and I had just started going to Winona's junior high school.

When I asked him how I was going to do it he said, "Well, you'll have to figure that out." That's pretty open-ended, especially to say to a creative kid like I was, but I didn't have any option because I had this bad habit – I really liked to eat, and during the middle of the day if you're not eating, you get awfully hungry before the end of the day. So I went a couple of days without eating and I went back to my dad again. I whined and I pleaded but he stood his ground and said, "No, you've got to do it. You've got to buy your own lunch and you'll find a way."

I did some menial things in the very beginning like yard work, pulling weeds, that sort of thing, got a couple of bucks and lunch was about a dollar a day back at that time. I ate sporadically, made the money last and disliked every minute of the manual labor I had to do in order to eat. However, when life closes one door it also opens a window somewhere. You just need to be engaged enough to see it and willing to climb through. So one day, I had a pack of gum and my friend Brian asked me for a piece. I knew how hard I had to work for the 25 cents it took to buy this pack of gum and I refused. He wanted a piece pretty badly and offered me a dime for it. It didn't hit me right away, and then all of a sudden, WHAM! It hit me!

I'm pretty quick with numbers and I figured that 25 cents is 5 cents a piece and he's going to give me a dime. I'm doubling my money. It was like fireworks or a huge light bulb turned on in my brain. That was one of my first entrepreneurial impulses. I sold him the piece of gum for a dime and ended up selling the other four pieces that same day.

Now I had that 50 cents plus a little bit of other money I earned, so on my way to school the next day I bought 10 more packs of gum. I sold them all and doubled my money again. I figured that because I was making a profit of 25 cents a pack times 10 packs, there would be enough money for my lunch, an ice cream bar, plus a little extra, and that I could do this every day. I felt like I had struck gold.

I started to develop an understanding of customer service and learning what types of gum certain people wanted. I would deliberately purchase that gum knowing that I would sell each person one or two pieces during the day. I kept all of this information in a small college-ruled composition notebook, which I now wish I had kept. I wrote customers' names, kinds of gum they liked, an accounting of how many pieces of gum I sold each day, and how much money I made each day – I had my own financial ledger.

After my dad would leave for work, I would gather my schoolwork and an empty duffle bag. I had to walk to school a little more than a mile and a half, but on the way I went to Ruprick's, a small grocery store, and buy whatever gum he had. At 10, 20, 30 packs a day, I quickly bought this store out of gum. I packed them into the duffel bag and then into my locker. I had a pocket full of change and kept much of my on-hand supply in my Trapper Keeper. It was fun and I felt like a millionaire. I was making $2, $3, $4, $5, sometimes as much as $10 a day. Do the math: 40 packs of gum is $10 a day. That is a lot of money for a small-town kid in 1982.

I lived too close to school to ride the bus. Initially I complained about walking to school because nobody would drive me there like the rich kids' parents drove them. But every negative can yield an equal or greater positive, when we are open-minded enough to see and creative enough to take advantage of the opportunity.

One very important point, and it was one of my earliest lessons, is whatever is illegal has a high profit margin. Gum was illegal to have in our junior high school. When you got caught chewing gum you had to spit it out, which actually worked out well for my business because the other kids knew they would just come right to me and I'd sell them another piece. My customers would get lunch money or an allowance from their parents and always seemed to be flush with dimes and quarters. After a couple of months, kids started calling me "Gumby."

I kept growing the business but eventually at around 40 packs a day I maxed out on what I could do alone. At the same time, some buddies who rode the bus to school wanted in, and they could sell to people I didn't know in their classes. What I ended up doing was my first lesson in learning to create an opportunity for other people to earn AND sell my product for me. I would source the product, or buy all the gum, from Ruprick's, Midtown Foods, and Erickson's Gas Station. When I got to school, I would sell it to them for 35 cents a pack. (Remember, I had only paid 25 cents.) They still made 15 cents profit per pack and were happy with that. I was now both a retailer and a wholesaler. They were unable to purchase the gum on their own because they rode the bus to school and their parents would have thought it quite strange if they purchased a bunch of gum and brought it to school. With a single parent who wasn't watching me that closely, I had free reign to develop my entrepreneurial skills. Plus, my dad told me to "find a way." So I learned right then how valuable it is to get other people selling for you and I made a consistent, safe profit.

At this time, I also learned the detrimental impact government can have when it gets involved and takes away your profits. The state of Minnesota started collecting a 6.5 percent sales tax on candy, so that bit into my profits significantly. Luckily, this occurred toward the end of my gum business' life.

One day in Economics class, the teacher was having us study

about securities (stocks, bonds, and the Stock Exchange system). He taught us how successful companies sold shares to investors to raise capital. I had no clue about these kinds of things because we never really discussed money in our house other than to save as much as possible. I was intrigued, and the more I learned about stocks the more I thought, "Well, I've already got a business, and I know that there are a lot of rich kids in my class." These were the kids who always had the name-brand pants that actually fit and weren't high-water hand-me-downs, like I had been wearing. These kids had the Nikes or Reeboks. They had CDs when they were first coming out and I still taped songs off the radio. Therefore, these kids always seemed to have some discretionary income and they didn't want to buy gum from me and sell it. They didn't need to, because they had other options, but they were perfectly willing to invest a little money. So I created shares of stock in my gum business and sold it to people for $10 a share. I divided up with them most, but not all, of my profits every week. Why did I need to raise more capital? Because I had bigger aspirations than simply selling gum.

Initially I was motivated only by hunger, and it eventually blossomed into a truly exciting and profitable venture. At this time, I used to read treasure magazines all the time and yearned to own a metal detector. My goal was to save up the $500+ to purchase my own White's metal detector. My dream was to be a millionaire and I thought that finding treasure would help me to accomplish this. Business was going really well and I was making good money. I was living high on the hog, able to eat whatever I wanted for lunch and saving money. I know my dad thought it was strange that I always had extra cash but he didn't ask too many questions.

1.3 The beginning of the end

Luckily I learned while very young that when you break the law, you will eventually get caught. My business had grown too big and we could no longer keep it under the radar. About five or six months after I began this enterprise, the vice principal got wind of what I was doing and called me into his office. He said he knew that I'd been selling gum and that teachers had reported how much gum I was selling. They had already searched my locker and found numerous boxes of gum. He demanded to know everything, but I would not reveal the names of my customers, partners, or investors. This landed me in a heap of trouble for a 12-year old. I thought I should have gotten praise or maybe some economics extra-credit but no, I just got in trouble.

Then he gave me a choice – expulsion for three days or two weeks worth of after-school detention. Neither option was acceptable. Expulsion went on my record and my dad would be notified. After-school detention lasted for 30 minutes, which meant I would not leave school until 3:30 p.m. My dad got home from work at about 3:40 everyday and expected me to be home when he got there. I could not make it home in 10 minutes after detention, so staying after school simply would not work.

I begged, pleaded, and finally SOLD him on why not to expel or give me after-school detention, but instead give me one month of detention during the lunch hour. I'd get a half hour for lunch and spend the first 15 minutes walking around with a five-gallon bucket to collect other kids' garbage. It was more humiliating than anything else and was very effective. However, I was being punished for something that I believe should have been celebrated. That summer, I bought my first White's metal detector and started my second business venture.

1.4   Trilogy of Freedom

I have spoken since 1989 to literally thousands of people about bettering their lives and I always ask folks the same basic questions.

What is your purpose in life?

Why do you believe you are alive?

What is your passion?

Why do you do what you do?

What goal would you be willing to do anything to accomplish?

Almost every time the questioning boils down to the root motivation of **personal freedom**. People I talk to consistently feel trapped, unhappy, unsettled, wanting for more, many without hope and some desperate to find a genuine shot to get what they want in life. So often they do not realize that they must make their own shot. Nobody is going to give you anything and, if they do, watch out for the strings.

I didn't find a shot at success – I created my own. Sales was my 1st step on my life's journey toward freedom – freedom of choice. When you have the ability to go to the grocery store and buy what you want rather than what you can afford, or when you go to a restaurant and order what you want and never look at the right side of the menu (at the prices), this is what I mean when I refer to the freedom and power to choose. I choose where I live, how I will raise my children, what vehicle I will drive, what kind of health coverage I will have, how often and how long I will vacation – I am in control of my life. I refused to trade my freedom for the perception of security, a J.O.B. Employers will pay you just enough so you do not quit and you will usually work just hard enough so they won't fire you. Until you become independent, you cannot live free. It all begins with making the decision as to what lifestyle you will live and commit to stop just earning a living. Someday you will die. But will you have lived or merely existed?

Until you make the absolute decision to be independent no matter how tough your freedom journey gets, I believe financially in our country you will not be free. Until you decide, someone else will decide for you. Your employer, mortgage company, spouse, parents, friends, and so many more will dictate how and when you do what you do. Sales sets you free – you control your income and therefore control where and how you spend it. Once you decide on your WHY and then learn HOW to create money, from where there was once nothing, NOBODY can take that away from you. The more you do it, the more confident you become, and the more people want to do business with YOU because of that confidence.

Build your experience and confidence and others will want to learn from you and then your income will be truly limitless. Sales first, then management, and finally leadership make up the trilogy of freedom. I learned these lessons by accident at age 12. How long will it take you? I saw how my dad allowed the railroad to control him and the factory controlled my step-mother. I learned what lifestyle I did not want by simply paying attention. I learned that in the U.S. there is a new millionaire every 126 minutes. This proves it is possible, and just because I was not a millionaire yet, did not mean it would not eventually happen. I also learned that more than 60 percent of the value of the roughly $750,000,000 worth of U.S. currency printed every day was in $100 bills – just because I did not have a pocket full of $100 bills did not mean the guy next to me didn't. If other people are becoming millionaires and have pockets full of cash, then it means I can too – I just had to learn how. I yearned in the pit of my stomach to enjoy the lifestyle of financially intelligent people, who knew how to make money from nothing instead of trading precious hours of life for dollars in a paycheck. I was passionate, relentless, stubborn, and determined to learn how to be free. I already had my "why" but I was missing the "how." I loved my family, but had to come to the hard realization that they could not teach me what they did not know. I had to find other role models who already were living the life I wanted.

Everybody's life is either an example to follow or a warning sign of what NOT to do. What is or is not an example or warning sign depends on your desired lifestyle and your current place in life. You must find someone who lives it, not just talks a good game. I saw and felt in my own family what it was like to exist paycheck to paycheck. Allowing an employer or bank to dictate my life was not for me. When people so often ask me why I do what I do, I answer, "Freedom." Whenever anyone has attempted to control me without my consent, I react viciously and always fight back. When it comes to my independence and freedom of choice, nothing will stand in my way.

I once toured the memorials in Washington D.C. and was deeply affected by the Korean War Memorial. I walked up on a sunny fall day and I saw it, the quote carved into the marble, "FREEDOM IS NOT FREE." It is our heritage to be free. So many have given so much so we may have this opportunity to live as we choose. Respect their sacrifice by becoming all you can be. Honor our country by living free. Don't trade it for anything – not a J.O.B., a new car, an expensive house, a vacation, or consumer junk.

Slavery supposedly ended after the Civil War. However, I see self-imposed economic slavery all around our great nation. I say self-imposed because the path to financial freedom is all around you. There are many examples of successful people to follow. Unfortunately, financial ignorance (to not know) and financial stupidity (to know and still make foolish decisions) are so easy. Financial foolishness is rewarded by praise for over-consumption using other people's money (i.e. credit cards, consumer loans, etc.). People may be impressed by your new Jaguar, but they do not think about how you are paying for it. Surround yourself with these people and you will remain broke. What will be the actual amount of money you paid for the Jaguar when the loan is paid off? How many hours of your life will have been traded, which you can never reclaim, so you can drive this momentary pleasure?

1.5 DEDFIL = Anti-Sheepitization™

To succeed, to be free, I learned you must understand and be willing to live by delayed gratification. Our immediate-gratification-based society and economy, which reward people for financially foolish decisions, is making financial slaves out of so many. Wait a minute, I am wrong. These people are not MADE to do anything; they chose to be financially stupid and will suffer as a result. Only by Developing Emotional Discipline, Financial Intelligence, and Leadership (DEDFIL™) skills, can you obtain financial freedom and keep it for a lifetime. I understand all too well that once you achieve freedom, keeping it is not guaranteed. Your IQ does not increase in direct proportion to your income. When you simply make a lot of money but lack either the intelligence or self-discipline to keep it, somebody will happily be there to take it from you. I started with nothing, made a lot, lost it all *plus some*, and then made it back again. To those who say money won't buy happiness, I say, "Neither will poverty. Which method of payment will you choose?"

My very first step to living financially free was deciding to do so. I simply would not settle for anything less, not in my business or personal life. My wife and I have had many spirited conversations about money and control over the years. These have gotten to where they don't happen any longer because we are now on the same financial team with a common goal of continuing to live free. In my business ventures, I do not strive to control people, and in turn I do not allow anyone to control me. I despise the label "employee". I strive to provide the information and tools so people can stop being sheeple, and lift themselves up. I call this Anti-Sheepitization™. Isn't it time you got up off of your knees and broke away from the herd? It is absolutely possible for you to live the lifestyle of your dreams when you are deliberate in your thoughts and actions. Life is not accidental and I do not believe in coincidence. Things happen for a reason and it is up to each of us to figure out "why", learn from it, adapt and persevere until we have what we want.

I learned the difference at age 19 between employee and independent contractor, and I knew I would never be an employee again. I would not allow the government to be paid first from MY labor and then I was allowed to keep whatever was left over. The government does not own my time, emotional energy, or experience – my personal productivity. It was my productivity that was traded for this wage but yet my needs came second to Uncle Sam's. This did not make sense to me. Employers tell you what to do, how to do it, and how much your time is worth. But as employees, sheeple accept that because of the perception of job security. Again, since when is security defined as prolonged poverty? Until you break free from being an employee, you cannot be truly free. Real money will not come from renting your time. It does however result from taking ownership of your own productivity.

Let me tell you a story. One day my primary lawyer and I were driving to an appointment. Seemingly out of the blue, Ed said to me how he envies me, which to say the least, surprised me very much. I intimately knew how much he earned, at least from me, since I paid his hourly fee. I asked him to explain and he said, "I may make a lot per hour but my income is limited by my time – I only have 24 hours in a day. I can raise my rates but only to a certain point. Otherwise clients will go to another attorney capable of doing the same job for less money. Allen, you have no limit to how much you can earn. You have taken what you learned, packaged it, and then sell it to others so they too can better their lives. You set them up in positions where they can make more money than anywhere else in their lives and you make a small amount off of what they generate. This way you have set yourself up to earn money 24 hours a day, seven days a week, 365 days a year no matter whether you are in your office or sitting on a beach in the Caribbean. That is why I admire you and what you have done."

I truly had never thought of it quite like that before. I was only 24 at the time and thought of him as the lucky one, but he was right. Because of my ability to sell, I was able to earn enough money to be free of needing a J.O.B. and as a result became desheepitized! In addition, I worked hard to develop my management skills so I could manage the details of a small business. Finally, I took my ability to sell a product and slowly developed my ability to sell ideas. My definition of leadership is simply the selling of your ideas. It takes the same skills as selling a product but you have to be better at it because you can touch, taste, smell, and see a product, but an idea is intangible, so the customer is really buying YOU. Even though there is a lot of money in sales, the big money is in leadership, but I will go into this in greater detail later in this book. The point here is – no matter how much money you earn per hour there is a limit to your earning potential – you will end up 6 feet under in a box some day, thus your time and emotional energy are limited.

Until you are in a position of ownership, in which your income is tied to performance, NOT time, and you develop emotional discipline, you will have a very hard time breaking free from financial enslavement. Everyday we are enticed with more than 5,000 advertisements, given easy access to other people's money, and then immediately rewarded with other people's praise and recognition for our new "whatever," that it is becoming increasingly difficult to not give in to the societal pressure of keeping up with the Joneses. I once heard money is just a game of debt: The more debt you owe the poorer you are, and because you are poor the harder you will have to work for everyone else other than yourself. However, the more people owe you, the richer you become. Learn the rules and strategies of the "money game". Then you can play too. It is your choice – play or be played! If you cannot do it for yourself, then think of the example you are setting for your children. Do you want them to struggle as hard as you have? What will be the true inheritance you pass on to them, to continue just being another of our economy's work horses? Children tend to mimic what they see, good or bad. They rarely do as my dad so often recommended, "Do as I say, not as I do." This never made any sense to me because I felt if it was good enough to tell me to do, shouldn't you do it, too? We lead by example whether deliberate or accidental. Whether we like it or not, we will be a positive example or a warning sign. I made a commitment early on that all the negatives of my childhood would absolutely stop with my generation. I believe that by making this commitment and sticking to it, no matter how tough times became, helped to build my character and confidence.

1.6   Lead by example and judge by results

Make the commitment to have the financial discipline to say, "NO, I do not *need* that right now." I committed to wait until my business could pay for that new car instead of renting my time to do so. I committed to INVESTING my time in self-development in order to be a better leader. I believe money is a result of actions taken, not a cause to act. This is why most people seem to hate their J.O.B., because they are only doing it to make money. Money only motivates most people up to the point their basic needs (clothing, food, shelter) are met. After that, people are driven by meeting their emotional needs (pride, respect, significance, etc.). Unless it is purely a temporary survival position, I will NOT work a J.O.B. just to make money. My life is too precious to me because I believe I will not get a second chance at living. I have committed to actually live my life instead of just exist through it from birth to death. I believe life will pay me in direct proportion to the number of people I help. Therefore, in order for me to get rich, I must first help a lot of other people to get what they want.

I started helping by selling them products they needed. Eventually I developed further and was able to lead people to help others, but you cannot put the cart in front of the horse. You must start out in the horse position pulling YOUR own cart (selling) and stop pulling your employer's cart by keeping your J.O.B. You will only get tired this way, and at the end of the journey, won't have much to show other than a bag of oats and some water. Because you were such a good horse, the employer will use you again for their next financial journey. How long can your legs and back continue to pull other people's carts before you finally say, "I have had enough!" and mean it?

When you learn to sell, you have taken ownership of your time. This was an amazing realization for me. It is my time, mine! Once I decided nobody could afford to rent it any longer, I began to learn the skills necessary to match my thinking with reality. I may think my time is valuable but until I am able to create something from nothing with my time, it is only valuable in my head and sadly that value will not pay the rent. I had to develop my sales skills so I could transfer my belief to other people. That is all that sales really is – the transfer of one person's belief in something to another person (effective communication). I believe that when you decide what your life will be, stop settling for anything less, then learn how to sell in order to make yourself financially free of needing a J.O.B., you have started on the Path of Performance. This is the path to enjoying your dream lifestyle instead of continuing to struggle just making a living.

I do not believe the struggle will get any easier until we take decisive, deliberate action. Why am I actually writing this book? Because I am concerned! I cannot help but see it every single day. I believe God gave us two eyes and two ears, but only one mouth for a reason – look and listen twice as much as you talk. I pay close attention and what I am seeing and hearing deeply concerns me. I have traveled enough outside the U.S. to see how valuable the middle-class is. There will always be the haves and have-nots but the middle class is, in my opinion, the most valuable sector of our society, the necessary stepping stone from poor to rich. Few will be able to simply leap from one day being poor to the next being rich. They need a middle ground. Many get there, like it, and stay, but in America I see evidence daily of the shrinking middle class. I believe the gap is widening dangerously between the rich and poor. I am NOT saying the sky is falling, but am stressing to everyone around me to either pay attention or be left behind. I don't fear change, but choose to study it, so I can create and seize the opportunities that change creates.

My ideal lifestyle has always been to live free – to be the type of person I would have admired as a child and adolescent. I need to be a successful businessman, husband, father, and civic leader – an example for others to follow. I decided to study and then develop myself in a very deliberate manner. I choose whom to follow and whom to align myself with. The person I eventually grew into, my level of personal satisfaction, happiness, pride, and the resulting income are not accidents. I do not believe life is accidental. We are here for a purpose and it is our personal journey to discover why we are here. My personal commitment to <u>constant self-development</u> was *essential.* Acceptance of <u>accountability for MY actions</u> was *critical.* Understanding <u>money's importance as a tool</u> while not being blinded by its allure was *stabilizing.* Realizing that <u>success at life is a team sport and it's OK to need other people</u> to help me along the way was *liberating.* Belief that <u>my future is not controlled by my past</u> was *empowering.* All were key elements to my being able to make my life's dream my everyday reality – that is what I decided and you can too! Everything I had experienced so far had been preparing me for and building up to Freedom Day (Wednesday, July 13th, 1988).

1.7   Truth # 1 Action Points

Anti-Sheepitization™, the belief and understanding that whatever lifestyle you desire to enjoy IS possible once you take ownership of your productivity. You CAN separate from the herd and break free from the other "sheeple." How do you make sure someone else does not pick your "typical way of life" for you?

A.   <u>Decide upon your ideal lifestyle.</u> What means the most to YOU? What must your life be/have so you feel fulfilled? Is it freedom, honor, pride, respect? Or is it relationships, income, net worth, car, house, children? There are NO wrong answers because it is YOUR life and you will occasionally revise your ideal lifestyle vision as you continue to grow, develop, and mature. The journey to enjoying your lifestyle will not begin until you decide on your direction.

B.   <u>Write your lifestyle decisions down on two small cards.</u> Laminate the cards and post one copy on your bathroom mirror so you have to see it at least once a day and carry the other one with you at all times to help you stay focused upon what really matters to you so you are able to keep up the good fight.

C.   <u>Review your decisions at least once every day.</u> Condition your brain to expect this ideal to become your eventual reality. You will not allow any other option to be available except what you have decided. Repetition is the mother of learning. This will revitalize your life's vision, clean your vehicle's windshield, so the picture of your future is crystal clear. Mental clarity of purpose is absolutely critical to success.

TRUTH # 2

Your past does NOT control your future,
unless YOU permit it to.

TM

2.1 Stop whining!

Let me start this chapter by emphasizing that we cannot change for the positive until we first face the truth. Winston Churchill said, "Men occasionally stumble upon the **truth**, but most of them pick themselves up and hurry off as if nothing ever happened."

I believe we have little if any control over what happens to us as children. We get the cards we are dealt, good or bad, and are forced by life to deal with them in the best way we know how. But that immediately stops when we become adults. At age 18 you are a man or woman, are old enough to go to war and die for what you believe in, and old enough to accept total accountability for your life. I believe that either you make it happen or allow it to happen to you. Until you face this obvious reality, I do not believe positive personal growth will occur. I speak to you only from a position of personal relevant experience.

2.2   Freedom Day

What I am about to tell you I do NOT tell you for sympathy, but to emphasize that I understand being in a tough desperate seemingly hopeless situation. As a child I lived in four foster homes. I was either witness to or personally experienced extreme examples of spousal abuse, child abuse, alcoholism, drug addiction, and many other horrible things that need not be mentioned here. When I was very young, I made a commitment to myself that these behaviors STOP at my generation. I was by far the oldest child and grandchild so I felt a huge responsibility to be an example of what life could be, instead of just perpetuating the warning signs by using the old excuse, "Well, this is what was done to me and it is all that I know." I was angry, confused, hurt and believed I was "damaged goods," but with this commitment I found the strength within to not make the same mistakes those around me did. It was not easy and I was very lonely for much of my journey to "right the ship." It really began to unfold on Freedom Day, when I turned 18, and immediately moved out of my parents' house.

July of 1988 was a gut-wrenching time for me, but exciting at the same time. This moment had been really building for nearly three years. When I was 15, my dad, who had been a single parent for close to six years, was getting remarried. As a result, my life became very difficult and I started a secret chart, a log that began at slightly more than 1,000 days, the number of days until I turned 18 and was free to leave and be on my own. Every single day, without exception, I crossed off a day. The pressure built as the numbers decreased. I believed that life would be better when I was able to make my own decisions, right or wrong. I would be able to be in control of my life. Many days were filled with arguments, and some were very vicious. I realize now, it takes two to tango, and I was a very challenging teenager to parent.

I did not want to let all the horrible things that had happened when I was younger be like water under the bridge, because what happened was wrong. Now more than ever, as a parent myself, I agree with how I felt as a teenager. The situation was a pressure-cooker that constantly had the heat being turned up and was ready to blow. Luckily, it didn't explode; thank God my dad and step-mother were strong enough not to quit on me and I did not quit on myself.

I share this with some hesitation but if it can help just one person, then it is worth it. In two different instances, I was prepared to take my own life, ready with instruments in hand, but thankfully did not follow through. I credit it to a belief that God had a better purpose for me (to help others), that life would be better in the future and if I did this it all ended without my even getting a chance to prove I was right. It may have been that keeping the log until Freedom Day gave me something to look forward to, or my sense of obligation to those family members younger than me not to give up. Who knows? The bottom line is, I am here and because of this strife, perhaps I have value to add to someone else's life. It is only by the intense pressure that a diamond is formed. Only in the extremes of hot and cold can steel be hardened and this is what life does to us all. I believe life will not challenge us more than we can endure, so I am constantly programming my mind that I must not give up, no matter what it takes. Together we can help others, but we must first start with ourselves.

Leading up to this big day, I had saved enough money to pay for one year of college plus two of the three quarters of living on campus. I did not have a clue where I would live the third quarter but believed I would figure it out when I got there. Immediately upon turning 18, I moved out and worked for six weeks before college began for my uncle building farm silos. It was very hard work, but I had achieved my freedom. I deliberately chose to attend the University of Minnesota's Duluth campus, the furthest I could get away from my family and still get in-state tuition. It was a clean slate, a new beginning, my chance to prove how right I was and wrong everybody else was. Shortly before I moved out, my dad bet me $50 that I would be back in six months or less. I did not care if I had to live in a box on a street corner; I was committed to NEVER moving back. I credit my dad for making me so mentally tough by making me so angry. Whether he did this on purpose or not, he was the source of much of my energy to continue the good fight and never give up. Failure was not an option, and because the only other option was to succeed, I went to work on the one thing that would be both my greatest asset AND my worst nightmare – my MIND!

2.3   Feelin' lucky?

In order to work on my mind, I had to separate from all things that I perceived to hold me back: family, many of my friends, and the environment in Winona. Little did I realize that the single largest piece of baggage I had to carry weighed only a few pounds and lived right between my ears. My mind helped me through the storms that IT often created. It was both a blessing and a curse, and fortunately I realized very quickly that either I needed to learn how to control it or it would control me. I would not choose to escape by using alcohol or drugs to numb the pain, or become obsessive in any of the other self-destructive behaviors I had seen so often growing up. No, escape was not an option. I had to face myself and deal with me.

When I went to Duluth in fall of 1988, I had very little self-confidence or self-respect. After you hear you are worthless and going to amount to nothing for so many years, deep down you do start to believe it. What you believe is your reality because you will make it so. I believed so many things that ended up not being true, but by believing them, I made them so. I acted in a certain way, and by repeating these actions, they became habits, and those habits became my character at the time. For example, I believed I was really not worthy of being loved or even being liked by other people my own age, so I would hide whenever possible. Thankfully I had a couple of friends who would not allow me to hide – Russ and Brian. They would drag me kicking and screaming out to parties. After a couple beers I began to loosen up and have fun. Brian would tease me relentlessly and because I was so defensive, I would fight back. He thankfully did not stop teasing and I softened. I learned that he was not attacking me but only kidding. I did not have to be on guard 24/7 around these guys. They accepted me for who I was and gradually I began to build my confidence.

People often make the mistake of seeing me in business now and think I have always been this confident. When I tell them stories like this, they find them hard to believe. I left the place and people I believed were dragging me down, and aligned myself sometimes on purpose and sometimes by accident with good people who elevated me and helped me to believe I could be more. I cannot thank Russ and Brian enough for what they did at the time. I am sure they did not have a clue how much they were helping me. How could they? Neither did I.

Your past is like yesterday's lunch – gone! Take from it but do not allow it to take from you. You control what your mind focuses upon, feels, believes, and ultimately what actions you take or don't. YOU!!! Eventually we all must stop blaming others for our current position in life. It is not my mother's fault, nor my dad's, nor my lack of a formal education, or race, or any other outside element's fault that I am in my current position – good or bad. I will neither blame my failures upon anyone else nor will I allow others to take the credit for my successes. However, I give great amounts of credit to the good people I have on my personal and business teams for the success I have enjoyed. Why? Because success is a team sport and I did not do it alone. It is because of their help that life is so sweet and the right thing to do is show great amounts of appreciation for the blessings I have earned.

Countless times I have heard those I encountered blame others for their misfortunes. Only when you stop blaming can you begin to grow. Blame accomplishes nothing and even if you have been wronged by bad people, they typically don't care, so the only person who sits and spins his wheels and gets nowhere is YOU. To give a destructive person such control over your present AND future is unacceptable. As an adult, you are where you are either because you made it happen or you permitted it to happen to you.

Often I hear that successful people are just lucky. I respond to these people with, "Luck is when opportunity meets preparation. Prepare yourself mentally and life will provide opportunities for you to seize. Don't prepare yourself and you will pass them by again and again." Successful people are not lucky. They are fortunate because they prepare their minds by studying other successful people, reading, and thinking proactively. They prepare their bodies with exercise and good diet. The mind and body are linked – that is undeniable. Physical actions speed mental results. To attempt to be mentally successful while physically unhealthy is like putting a brand new engine into a rusted-out shell of a car. The engine might run well, but when the body breaks down, it won't matter.

2.4   OK, in ya go!

I have had a lot of challenges with depression. I have tried prescribed medication and herbal supplements, professional counseling, and even hypnosis to "fix" the problem. For years I battled with the extreme highs and lows, but could never seem to overcome the need to hide and shut off the world for weeks on end. This was very destructive to my business and personal lives. Fortunately I was given a partner, my wife, who stuck with me no matter what. Imagine not getting out of bed for more than a week other than for necessities, avoiding phone calls, not answering the door, just shutting everyone out. It then begins to magnify because you begin to feel guilty for not living up to the ideal life you had created for yourself, but nothing you do seems to help. Sadly, few people understand how dark the place you are in actually is unless they have lived it.

What frequently snapped me out of it was pure financial necessity, which only lasted until the money once again began to flow. In a way, my financial success fueled the fire. You see, money will NOT change you and anyone who thinks that it will is wrong. Money provides the freedom to be more of what you already are deep inside. Money is an amplifier – the good gets better and the bad gets much worse. When you don't have a boss to be accountable to, you have to be accountable to yourself and if you are screwed up, who is going to get you back on track?

This is why having a trusted coach and routine are so critical to long-term success. Money provided me the freedom to be more of what I already was inside, and my bad side got worse and worse until I was forced to pull in the reins. This was a vicious cycle of extremes for years until I sought out and finally found the only "cure" that literally worked 100 percent of the time without exception.

I was allowing my past emotional crutches to creep into my brain because I had made enough money to have free time. During my free time, the little voice in my head, or as I sometime call it, "the itty-bitty shitty committee," was saying all of the horrible things to me that I had heard over and over as a child. Money did not make me happy, but it gave me the ability to seek out the answer and the time to deal with it. Without money, I would not have been able to control my past and eventually overpower it, so I could stop wasting precious time being depressed. I had a life to build which is much like laying a hardwood floor, and I knew money was but one single plank in the floor. While living in Miami, Florida in 2001, I realized I had to take control of this depression.

Because of my commitment to my lifestyle I found Zoltan Zenda, the single best personal trainer I have ever had the pleasure of being beaten up by every day for four months. He taught me how to set realistic goals, eat properly and exercise effectively. He supervised my efforts, held me accountable, and most of all, was an example to follow. He was not perfect, but he lived what he preached. I admired that he did not repeat my father's admonishment to do as he said, not as HE did. Because I admired him, I listened, learned, and grew healthier than ever.

Right before he pushed me to do one more set, he would always say, "OK, in ya go!" This was like a rallying call to dig deep and push harder. After about two months, I walked into the gym at 6 a.m. on a Monday and he immediately asked, "Allen, what did you eat this weekend?" Before I could answer, he asked, "How many doughnuts did you eat?" I have a weakness for Krispy Kremes and I sat down the day before and ate a half-dozen of the glazed with chocolate and sprinkles (my favorite). The amazing thing is, he could tell! I was not just another paycheck to him as I had been to other trainers. He actually cared enough to pay attention AND he had the skill necessary to spot such a change in me. This made me believe in him even more. That is a great trainer, and what I learned from Zoltan has served me well and will continue to do so for the rest of my life. I cannot thank him enough for being as great as he was at what he did – he specialized!

Quite by accident I began to notice how I felt and that it had been months since I had fallen into my "funk." I had discovered what was for me the single best cure for depression ever – proper diet and exercise. This may not work for everyone, but it can't hurt.

So the bottom line is, stop blaming others. You have the power to control your focus, thus your outcome. It is not your parents' fault you are broke. It isn't because you lack a college education; I dropped out after my freshman year. Your employer is not your problem. When you are ready to grow and move forward, to truly take a gigantic step toward living the lifestyle of your dreams, go to your local store and buy a small pocket mirror. Every time you find yourself beginning to feel sorry for yourself, creating excuses to justify your current lack of success, whining about how rough you had it, searching for a new method of escape, or blaming others for your position in life, pick up the mirror and look into it. What you will see is both your problem and your solution. And until you believe this, nobody can help you, because you can lead a horse to water, shove its head in the river, but you still cannot force it to drink. The river of time does not flow in reverse. You will get older until you stop breathing – this is an absolute. Just because you age does not mean things will get better.

Imagine you are floating down the river of time on a canoe. Most people I come across bounce like a pinball from rock to rock. They react to life instead of deliberately ACTING to take control of their lives. They whine the whole way down the river about what other people have instead of simply looking down and realizing there is a paddle right in front of them. The river may not stop, it may not flow in reverse, but by God, I can use this paddle to control my direction. Other people can speed you up by helping you, or slow you down by throwing obstacles in your path but only YOU can change your direction in life. Only the person in the mirror truly has that power. What are you going to do with your paddle?

2.5   Truth # 2 Action Points

History should be studied but not relived. Fortunately, with your knowledge and practice, you no longer have to drive only using the rearview mirror. You can lift your head high, look through the clear windshield to the future ahead and excitedly begin moving toward your ideal lifestyle vision. How do you get your past to serve you, to take from it, and stop its taking from you?

A.   <u>Decide your past is dead and gone and will no longer be allowed to limit you</u>. Your past has no power over your present or future other than what you give it. It is there to SERVE you only as a reference point for where you have been, not an indicator of where you are going!

B.   <u>Study your past for patterns of success</u>. You do not have to reinvent the wheel or come up with a magic answer, because inside you already exists examples of successful behavior. What has driven you before will drive you again, just like pressing the 7 key on your calculator will get a 7 over and over. Discover your hot buttons, your root emotional driving forces, and write them down in your journal. Why did you succeed when most people just quit? These are your own emotional keys to unlock the mystery of how to control your feelings by deliberately directing your emotional energy. When you know what you NEED, it is much easier to position yourself to get it.

C.   <u>Break your mental shackles by eliminating your patterns of failure</u>. Every obstacle you encounter on your journey is an opportunity for you to grow. Growth means change. Any time you feel weighed down, do whatever you must to change your emotional state. Whenever you begin to feel down, use an inspirational song, poem, book, or movie (whatever works for you). Do this over and over and your past's hold on you will gradually lessen, because your negative patterns will die and be replaced by positive, constructive visions of your ideal lifestyle. Life has rhythms, ups and downs. All positions are temporary, so do not beat yourself up when you get down. Just change your mindset. To get down on yourself is not productive and life only pays on results!

TRUTH # 3

Your mind is your greatest asset.

The sun rises upon a fresh new day as you stand there looking out over a field. Taking in this moment, you ask yourself many questions...

How fertile and nourished is this soil?
Does it get enough rain or will it need to be irrigated?
Has the field suffered any damage?

What crop will grow best, if anything?
What will grow if nothing is deliberately planted?
What will we do to keep it free from destructive forces?

Who will care for it?

This field is your MIND. You must ask and answer these and many more questions in order to take control of your most precious asset.

3.1 General Paul Sherman

In central California lies the Sequoia National Park, where conditions are perfect for an unbelievable growth opportunity. At the southern tip of the Sierra Nevada mountain range, among the majestic granite monoliths, glacier-torn canyons, roaring whitewater, and lush meadows grows the world's largest tree – nicknamed General Sherman. From a simple seed planted more than 2,000 years ago this giant has emerged. It has survived countless fires, storms, and droughts to remain standing strong for the world to see. In 1978 a branch fell to the ground, and this single branch was larger in diameter than the trunk of almost every other tree in the entire eastern United States!

What set of amazing circumstances had to be put in place for this tiny seed to grow into a mighty sequoia? I asked Paul, whom I have been coaching since November 1993, "What is the difference in your life now versus back when you started with me?" When he came to me, he was broke, both financially and in spirit. The world had kicked him in the groin again and again and I could see it. He was a single parent, had just lost his job because of discrimination, and was on the verge of losing his house.

I started him in a sales position on 11/11/93, paid solely on commission, and we have been working together ever since. He did not have any prior sales experience, at least not professionally, but I saw potential in him that he did not even see. I knew I had a sequoia seed to plant, the skill of sales with its limitless potential to change lives for the better, but at that time it seemed that Paul's mind has self-imposed limits much like the size limitations of a five-gallon bucket. His confidence was low and he ran from his problems instead of facing them head on. If you plant a sequoia seed in a small container, the tree will only grow to the size of its container's limits.

However, what I saw in him was great potential. He possessed qualities that you simply cannot teach someone – integrity, loyalty and heart. I believed that with the right MINDSET, he would grow into a powerful force to be reckoned with, and I was right. He just needed someone to tell him he could, show him a genuine path to success, and coach him along the way.

Even though Paul was given absolutely no guarantee of pay unless he sold, he accepted the position and began to learn how to sell. He told me years later that he took the position and accepted the risk of losing everything to start a new career at age 41 because he realized that he needed a change. What he had been doing so far, working for an hourly wage for somebody else, renting his time until they did not need him any longer, was not working out so well. To continue doing this would jeopardize his son's future, and that was unacceptable. He knew he had to learn a different path, but had not a clue what that path would be, so he began to search.

At the beginning he was only able to get sympathy sales. Gradually, as his mindset improved, he began to think like a success. His results began to match his thinking and became better and better, until he opened his own business working with my primary company at the time. Now he undertook a new adventure, how to manage a small business and earn his income from leading other people to sell. The ability to sell a product is one skill, but to sell your intangible ideas about why people should believe in you takes confidence, character, and guts. Paul came to me with character and guts and with a great deal of work on both of our parts, his confidence grew to the point it became humorous. He would walk into a conference room filled with people and say loudly so everyone could hear, "Ain't I great!" From beaten down to on top of the world, with an income to match, in only a matter of months – HOW?

I worked every day teaching him the exact truths explained in this book. I was only 23 years old when Paul approached me looking for help. I had experienced some success and certainly had overcome numerous personal obstacles, but I did not have anything fancy to dangle in front of him to motivate him. What drove him was his intense NEED to succeed. He did not <u>hope</u> to make a sale or <u>want</u> to own his own business; he NEEDED it in his soul and had no option other than to succeed. He did not have a safety net to catch him. If he failed, both he and his son would be living on the street. Paul grew into an impressive salesperson, inspirational speaker, motivational leader, and loyal business partner. He said that applying what I taught him helped him finally stop accepting mediocrity in his life. All he really needed was someone to believe in him and show him the path. By developing his mind, the sequoia seed I planted took root in a limitless fertile field and has grown into another General Sherman. Now 14 years of personal growth later, he lives on his ranch with his wife, multiple horses, and swimming pool – his ideal lifestyle.

3.2   Homeless at 18

What really is the difference between the bum on the street corner, offering to squeegee your window using God knows what while begging for spare change, and the multi-millionaire driving his fancy Lincoln to the office? They both have the same 24 hours in a day. This is one of the most important questions I ever asked myself. I knew I did not have the answer because I was a college dropout making $3.85 per hour waiting on tables at a Duluth, MN pie shop called Plush Pippin, so I began to seek out those who did. I decided to see the opportunities that are all around me instead of closing my mind and wallowing in my sorrows, so I searched. I have always believed that if your pile of money is bigger than mine, it means you know something I do not know and I am willing to do whatever it takes to get you to teach me how you earned that money. But before I could start learning to be rich, I needed a place to live.

It was February 1989, third quarter of my freshman year at college. I had a job, but $3.85 per hour gross before taxes was just not enough to pay for on-campus student housing. If you recall, I came to Duluth with enough money to pay for one year of tuition and books but only two quarters of on-campus housing. I had a dilemma, but fortunately I had joined a fraternity, Alpha Phi Omega, a few months prior. Those guys had a house known simply as 1818, and if you have ever watched the movie Animal House, that was 1818. Picture a three-story house with a basement, built around 1900. It had matted-down green shag carpet in the living room, a kitchen floor you could not walk on with stocking feet or your socks would stick to the floor and pull off, a foot of mold growing on the shower curtains, and the wonderful smell throughout the house of old cheap beer spilled during the almost nightly parties. All the available rooms were full and you needed seniority to even be considered to be allowed to move in, and I was a newbie. I needed a cheap place to live because I had no family to fall back on. There was no calling home for money. In Duluth, where it can get to 50 degrees BELOW zero in the winter, not having a roof over my head was not an option.

I believe that in some instances it is better to ask for forgiveness than permission. So I went to the house and looked for an opportunity to get in. I saw only one option. There was a single room in the basement. It did not have a door. The dark brown paneling had holes the size of basketballs. There was no working overhead light, and the 21 empty beer kegs currently stored there made it hard to find room to sleep, but that didn't matter because I did not have a bed This room was where Hawkeye, the official frat mascot, lived. So what did I do? I moved the kegs out, hung a trouble light from a nail on the ceiling so I could see, and then raked, yes raked, Hawkeye's dog hair off of the carpet so I could use my sleeping bag and be an official squatter in my new home.

When the other guys realized what I had done, I pled my case and SOLD them on letting me stay for $75 per month rent. One final thing I forgot to mention. The basement was not heated. The east wall of the house faced Lake Superior and because the hills are like those in San Francisco, that wall was exposed to the winter winds from the lake. Sometimes it got so cold that my shampoo and toothpaste would freeze. I eventually built a door out of 2 x 4's and bought a waterbed so the excess heat from the bed could warm the entire room. None of these hardships really mattered to me because I was FREE and I was self-sufficient and did not have to ask family for anything. Now that I had overcome homelessness, I went back to the business of becoming rich.

3.3 Restraining order anyone?

Mindset is the **field** itself and learning a skill is planting a seed in that field. My mindset was that of a *can-do* and a *need-to* person. I believed I must find a way to overcome my obstacles. I would not allow anyone or anything to hold me back. This was my decision and a promise made to myself. Because I have to live with myself for a very long time and look at my face in the mirror every day, I did not want to look at a liar. But all the motivation and drive in the world is not enough if you don't know **how** to get rich. If you get lost while driving to your desired destination in life, should you drive faster to fix the problem? Of course not, but I see it every day. Paul stopped when he was lost, asked for directions, and sought out a NEW more successful way to think and view the world. Sheeple just continue to do what they have always done, work harder in their chosen vocation, complain about it to anyone who will listen, and hope for positive changes to occur. They do the same things over and over but expect a different result and that is the definition of insanity.

What I did to learn how to become rich was a little out of the ordinary. But then again I believe if you want to enjoy a different sort of lifestyle, you must do different sorts of things. I thought that rich people dressed in expensive clothes, worked in office buildings, and drove expensive cars. I was partially right. Many rich people live this way but so do many people who are in debt up to their eyeballs, and when I was 18 years old I did not know the difference. However, I learned from both because some were examples and others warning signs of future doom.

Anyway, as funny as it sounds, during the spring and summer of 1989, I just walked up to nicely dressed people on the street and asked them if they were successful. Did they make more than $100,000 a year? At the time, that was big money in my mind. What was their job? How did they learn to be so successful? I asked a ton of other out-of-the-ordinary questions. I even approached cars, got the drivers to roll down their windows and asked them the same questions as they waited at traffic lights. Many just glared at me but a few actually took the time to talk to me. I learned so much that I decided to quit college. After talking to my frat brothers, some of whom had graduated, I learned they had a huge amount of debt and still were starting out in entry-level positions, if they could even find a job. I had no desire to owe $40,000 or more and then not be able to be debt-free until my late 20's or early 30's. Plus I came to believe that college only teaches you how to work for someone else. You do not need a college degree in order to succeed in my chosen field – being an entrepreneur. Business is *effective people-relations.* The person who buys a product from me really does not care if I have a formal education or not, just that I will do what I say I will when I say I will.

3.4   Mindset of the Rich

I asked many rich people how to become rich, and I listened for patterns. Fortunately, I found many and they are the truths this book and my life are built upon. Here are some of the gems I was given, specifically pertaining to mindset:

1. You must want it more than anything else and be willing to do anything to get it.

2. Believe in yourself no matter how dark the days appear or how many people say you can't do it.

3. Never take NO for an answer. There is always a way.

4. Focus on your objective with tunnel vision. All negativity must roll off of you like water off a duck's back. You cannot allow it to stick in your mind or else it will slow you down.

5. Your mind is the one place nobody can touch unless you allow them. They cannot make you happy, sad, or angry without your permission.

6. High expectations = High rewards. Shoot for the stars because life is short.

7. Even the worst day working for yourself is better than the best day working for someone else.

8. Never give up. If you do, you will never know how close you might have been to your dreams.

9. A brave man dies but once – a coward dies a 1,000 times. The worst pain in life is the pain of regret, so do not fear taking a risk, because there is no reward without risk.

10. Get an education in people studies. A college education is not necessary to be successful at business, just the ability to relate effectively to people. To learn this you

must be on the street. Go to the school of hard knocks and gain street smarts.

11. You can make money with your brain or your brawn. Your brain will not wear out. It will only get stronger with confidence and experience.

12. All education costs something, so be willing to pay whatever price is required.

13. Focus on learning every day – that is the most important! Be a green piece of fruit because the ripe fruit falls from the tree and rots on the ground. The master is constantly learning while the amateur already knows it all.

14. Trial and error get you experience and experience builds confidence. Confidence builds bank accounts.

15. Accept accountability for your own actions. Most problems only exist in your head. Don't run from problems. Rename them challenges and overcome them. God won't give you more than you can handle.

16. Specialize. Do only what adds to your physical, mental, and/or financial bottom line. If you don't enjoy it or it doesn't help you get where you want to go, then pay someone else to do it. Do not be a jack of all trades. To become rich you do not have time to do it all yourself.

17. Your focus must be upon helping other people get what they want in order to become rich. Be of service to others and the rewards will follow.

18. To become rich you must own your own productivity and get paid based upon what you produce.

19. The person with integrity, honor, and loyalty who genuinely seeks to benefit others will always win over the long term.

20. The right attitude will allow you to see the opportunity amongst the challenges.

21. Be deliberate in your thinking and speaking because success is not accidental.

22. Use whatever emotion you feel to drive your mind so you keep on moving forward. Negative emotions work only for short bursts. Your positive internal driving force will make you want to win every day. Use whatever works for the short run, but search for your life's purpose as you mature.

23. Sales is life's level playing field. In sales, everyone has the same shot because all you are judged on is performance. Never stop practicing how to sell better.

24. All increases in income are always preceded by moments of personal growth.

25. Your IQ does not increase in direction proportion to your income. Never forget where you started from or who helped you along the way, otherwise you are destined to return back to where you began.

3.5 Excuses are like ...

I guarantee you I am not the biggest, strongest, smartest, or richest competitor on the field of life. I also guarantee that in the competition of life, I will win. I will outlast everyone else. No one will push more, run longer, or fight harder. Winning is in my blood now. To lose is simply not an option. The only way anyone will beat me is if they knock me out with a lucky punch or I am dead. Victory in life goes to those who simply will not give up, they outlast everyone else. Life is not a sprint but a marathon and what you need most is HEART. You cannot keep a person with heart down for long.

This is how I think, and why I have won more than I have lost in life so far. I do not play the game of life to tie. At the end of this game we will all end up six feet under in a box. I will win or die striving – period! I believe this is also how you must think in order to win. The game is always won or lost before it has even begun because whoever has absolutely committed to winning will win. Never forget that both winning and losing are habits and bad habits can be broken with the right mindset. Paul and I developed our confidence over time and with that confidence, right or wrong, we thought we were invincible. When you think you are a winner on the inside, your life on the outside begins to mimic that. You must be a millionaire in your mind long before your bank statement will show the money. Money is a result, not a cause. Life's rewards come as a result of training your brain to think and your body to act successfully.

I have learned by my coaching efforts over the years, that sheeple subconsciously give themselves a built-in excuse to justify their failure before they have even entered the arena to compete. When you use certain words, which I call "Glass Words", such as; *if, try, hope, hopefully, wish, can't, possibly, maybe, problem*, you set yourself up for failure. What you are doing is expecting to fail and trying to lessen or soften the pain caused by your failure to produce. You have options when you use these words and failure is one of those options you are allowing yourself to choose. When you don't accomplish what you set out to do, you can always then say, "Well, at least I tried." Is this what you want them to carve into your tombstone? "Here lies John. Born _____. Died _____. At least he tried." When you communicate, be **deliberate** and replace Glass Words with Concrete Words. You can easily convert them. For example, if becomes WHEN, hope becomes NEED, problem becomes CHALLENGE, and try becomes STRIVE. The words you speak are outside examples of what is going on inside your mind.

When you commit and stand your ground, you gain pride, self-empowerment, and respect that nobody can take away from you. When you truly commit to do something, an amazing thing happens. Instead of your brain searching for a new excuse to justify your current position, it will search for ways to get the goal done. My grandmother was a tough woman who did not pull any punches. She said to me many times when I was very young, "Excuses are like assholes, everyone's got one and they all stink! Allen, if you only spent half the time doing the job that you spent whining and making excuses, you'd be done by now." This lesson is my inheritance from her. Life pays on results ONLY and the people who find a way to overcome whatever is put in their path and still produce get paid. I do not just mean money – life has many ways of paying us (love, respect, health, appreciation, happiness, pride, and finally money). Commit to your desired lifestyle, no matter what, until you are able to LIVE it, for this is nothing less than being free to choose your way. It took 13 years of blood sweat and hard work, but thankfully now I live my desired lifestyle every day. Success is not easy, but it sure is worth it.

3.6   Can YOU handle the truth?

Everybody works hard but most still just get by – why? MINDSET! In recent years especially, I have often asked, "How is the classic all-American family supposed to make it in today's world?" They seem to allow everyone to control and rip them off and don't even get angry about it any longer. It is the same as the frog in the pot. Put the frog in boiling water and it immediately senses the drastic change in temperature and jumps out. If you put him in cool water and slowly turn up the temperature, it won't even sense the temperature difference, or by the time it does it will be too late. How is this any different from the person who thinks the $500 credit card debt is no big deal, makes the minimum payments after he purchased the new TV he just had to have, then takes out a car loan, mortgage, financed home improvements, and on and on. By the time he realizes what is happening, it is too late and he is cooked! He is trapped in the cycle that sucks the life out of our fellow Americans – work hard, pay the government, get your paycheck, pay your debts, and live on whatever is left over (if anything is left).

Until you take control of your productivity, this is your vicious circle of despair, your financial hamster wheel. Before you know it you will be old, tired, drained, and broke but you will have made other people money. The people controlling the dial on the stove are the ones who benefited from your time, emotional energy, and experience. They live well off of your lack of emotional discipline, financial stupidity, risk avoidance, and absence of leadership. Your lifestyle is your responsibility. Your reading this book is not an accident. It is a wake-up call. When you are ready to be honest with yourself sit, think, and ask yourself, "What option do I really have?" Your life will not improve until *you* improve. The man screamed at life, "Give me more time!" And life replied, "Give me more of YOU." Life will pay you exactly what you demand from it – nothing more and nothing less.

Back to the question – "How is the classic all-American family supposed to make it in today's world?" This question inspires me to ask many more, such as:

1. Why do you willingly work for the government from January through mid-May? Why do you allow your own government to presume it owns your productivity first and take almost half of your wages before you get to use

your income for your own family?

2.   Why do we allow our government to lie to us and push one generation's problems onto the next instead of facing them head-on and finding a solution? Do you really believe anyone younger than a Baby-Boomer will get back even dollar for dollar what they have paid into Social Security? Why do we continue to pay into what is in essence becoming just another Ponzi scheme?

3.   Why do we as a people tend to listen to each other's whining and excuses instead of helping to elevate each other through tough love and hard work?

4.   What are you really passing on to your children and grandchildren?

5.   Why have you accepted that the classic picture of one parent working while the other stays home raising the children is now considered a LUXURY which fewer and fewer believe they can afford?

6.   Why are we not noticing that the world is smaller and more financially competitive than ever before? If we don't get our American financial house in order, the other stronger, more competitive, hungrier and more efficient nations WILL take over economically, and the idea I was raised with, *America is and will always be # 1*, will be replaced with merely talking about how great we once were.

I have so many other sharp questions like these, far too many to list here because I believe these are enough to make my point. As Winston Churchill said it, "The **truth** is incontrovertible. Malice may attack it, ignorance may deride it, but in the end, there it is." My life-coach likes to say, "You may as well start with the truth because you will end with it." Sales IS the art of honest, effective communication. By asking thought-provoking questions, using personal integrity and unrelenting perseverance, you can help people and get paid well. Sales is a necessary part of life for those who choose not to be ostriches and bury their heads in the sand while pretending everything is OK. Sales is a crucial part of effective leadership, and now more than ever leadership is what our families, businesses, and our nation need most. True leaders are willing to stand up, do and say what is right, no matter how tough it may be.

We are all already capable of being great at sales. Many of you are sales pros and do not even realize it. Look at our children and how they use every tool in their mental arsenal to get what they want. We have all been great at sales, but many have been distracted for so long earning a living, they have forgotten how. If you have ever received a raise at a job, you can sell! If you have gone out on a second date with the same person, you are either good at sales or have been sold by someone better! If you are married, have talked another human being into spending the rest of their life with you, then you are absolutely fabulous at sales! Sales is not hard. For us to become stronger, a better example for others around us to follow, we must learn how to sell and practice this skill in our everyday lives. With the ability to effectively sell our beliefs to others, we will never want for money or any of the other wonderful things life has to offer. We can help those around us stop being sheeple, but we have to start with ourselves first.

I believe each of our households is a business and should be run like one and I have long lived by the belief that my objective is not to build my business. Instead I will focus upon building my people up (spouse, kids, customers, and friends) and they in turn will build the business. I have made it part of my lifestyle to build by helping others build. The more people I can help to live free, the freer I will be able to live. Successful people create more; they do not just take in order to become whole.

Fortunately, all positions in life are temporary, whether they are up or down. This is both a word of encouragement to the poor, and of caution to the rich. You can change your position in life by changing your mindset. What you think about most is what your reality will become. Stop allowing yourself to be Sheepitized. You have the power to take control and develop exactly the lifestyle of your dreams by applying this information. I believe in the adage, "If it ain't broke don't fix it" but if you are broke financially and/or emotionally then there needs to be some fixin' goin' on.

You do not have to live within your current means and sacrifice forever. Instead, learn how to expand your means to fit your desires. This starts with properly preparing your field. Until you have the mindset of a winner your field will not be ready for good seeds to take root and grow. When they do begin to grow you must watch over them and remove the weeds (the negative thoughts/people and limiting beliefs). If left unchecked, weeds will eventually take over and kill the good seeds, even those of the mighty sequoia tree. Manage your mental garden well and the fruits you harvest as you journey through life will be bountiful. You will reap what you sow!

3.7 Truth # 3 Action Points

Your mind is such an amazing gift. No longer will your greatest asset be allowed to be used against you. You understand the truth now, that learning to control your mindset is the only real path to success. Because you have decided, now your ideal lifestyle is only a matter of time and effort. It will happen because all positions are temporary, and NOW is your time to shine. How will you ensure that your mind helps you live as you choose from this point on?

A. Prepare for planting by opening your mind to the opportunities around you. This is a skill that must be developed. See what others miss. When you see an opportunity to help solve someone else's challenge (problem), develop a creative solution that will get you paid. Remember, not all payments are in dollars.

B. Keep your field free of weeds by whatever means necessary. Limiting beliefs and negative people all attempt to plant potentially destructive weeds in your field. YOU control your mindset by protecting it against the inevitable infestation attempts from weeds. You control what gets planted and what is allowed to grow, so choose wisely to what and whom you will listen. Be willing to push away everything and everyone who attempt to hold you back, drag you down, or destroy your good seeds. This is NOT a one-time thing. It must be done constantly because weeds are ALWAYS trying to take root.

C. Never stop nourishing your crops and expanding your field's size. Your mind is a limitless expanse. Learn from other people who have been there and done what you are setting out to do, by any means possible. Use meetings, videos, books, audio CDs, it does not matter, but never stop feeding your brain. Your mind's and body's growth are only limited by what you know and how you feel. Learn to grow and grow to learn. Apply your knowledge and a bountiful harvest is assured because every increase in income is preceded by a moment of personal growth.

STEP 1

Where Have You Been?
Summation of Action Points

Truth # 1
Decide what YOUR lifestyle will be,
or someone else will!

A. Decide upon your ideal lifestyle.
B. Write your lifestyle decisions down on two small cards.
C. Review your decisions at least once every day.

Truth # 2
Your past does NOT control your future,
unless __YOU__ permit it to.

A. Decide your past is dead and gone and will no longer be allowed to limit you.
B. Study your past for patterns of success.
C. Break your mental shackles by eliminating your patterns of failure.

Truth # 3:
Your mind is YOUR greatest asset.

A. Prepare for planting by opening your mind to the opportunities around you.
B. Keep your field free of weeds by whatever means necessary.
C. Never stop nourishing your crops and expanding your field's size.

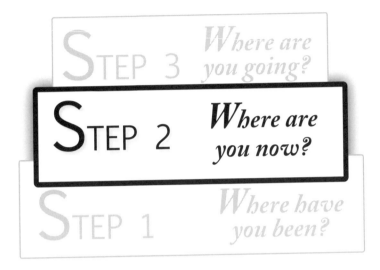

STEP 3 *Where are you going?*

STEP 2 ***Where are you now?***

STEP 1 *Where have you been?*

With a clear awareness of your present position on your life's journey, along with an understanding of WHY you are here, you can make an informed decision as to the direction to take in order to live the lifestyle you desire. There is nothing more important to future achievements than taking the right direction.

Use the information within the next three truths to better understand your present and more effectively channel your efforts. Move forward deliberately and a life filled with freedom and prosperity awaits.

TRUTH # 4

To get there,
first you must know your starting position.

In order to make a journey you need to know exactly where you are going AND from where you are starting. I decided upon my desired lifestyle, and had a detailed specific destination point. However, I really was never very clear about how critically important it was to thoroughly understand my origination point...in other words, where are you starting from right now?

Let us say your ideal lifestyle is metaphorically the same as Denver, Colorado. When you get into your vehicle, which direction are you going to drive? East, west, north, or south? If you believe your start point is Chicago, then you would simply begin to head west, but what if you actually were in Dallas or even worse, Las Vegas? Heading west would not do you much good at all. The likelihood of ending up in Denver would be slim to none. You would wander until you ran out of supplies and died or became discouraged and gave up. This is what so many I have seen over the years have done. And once you quit the first time, it gets easier and easier to quit again and again.

Both quitting and persevering are habits, as are losing and winning. You must properly prepare for this life journey. I was once told that if I had three days to chop down a tree, I should spend the first two days sharpening my axe. For you to travel from where you are NOW, you must complete a detailed personal inventory and do as much mapping as possible to determine your best route.

Success is NOT accidental. Successful people did not just wake up one morning and find out they had arrived. There is not a cruise ship or a first-class airplane ride in which you just get to sit back and be the passenger in the journey to your ideal lifestyle. Successful people are that way because they think and act like other successful people. Because of their actions, they will develop lifelong habits that gradually become their character. All of this adds up to enjoying their dream life.

4.1 Before you leave, three main questions must be answered

1.   Which vehicle will you drive? A Yugo or Lincoln? An SUV, a Volkswagen bug, or a luxury RV? The **vehicle** you take on this journey is the method you will use to make money (J.O.B., owning a business, real estate, marrying a rich spouse, burglarizing houses, inheriting money, winning the lottery, etc.). What kind of a vehicle do you currently use? Do you even have one? Is it weak and about to fall apart while on your journey? What can you do to strengthen your current vehicle until you trade it for one that is better?

If you own your own business that functions without you having to run it and you just collect a check once a month, then you have a fast, well-tuned race car and can get to wherever you want quickly. If you are working as a busboy for $3.85 per hour and using much of the rest of your time to go to college so you could learn to get a better paying J.O.B., then I believe your vehicle is slow at best and may never get you further than the edge of the town you are in. The vehicle you choose is crucial, not just to your speed, but your comfort along the way, whether you can afford to stop and sleep in a hotel or rolling up in the back seat. Can you stop to eat when you are hungry, or must you wait because your vehicle simply does not provide you any extra for necessities like food? Rich people are rich because the vehicles they use to get what they want are fast and powerful!

2. How much **fuel** do you have in the tank? This is your current financial position. Are you broke and may have to hitchhike for the first few miles? Do you have a $1,000,000 trust fund from which you can draw interest for extra security if you need it? Or are you somewhere in the middle, like most people, and living hand-to-mouth, paycheck-to-paycheck? How will you keep the tank full?

Learning accounting, along with reading a balance sheet and income statement were foreign subjects to me when I started. But you need to know where you are, how much you have, how much you owe, to whom, and at what interest rate. When I started I did not have much debt because I did not spend more than I earned. However, my girlfriend, now my wife, came with a lot of school loans and consumption debt and I attacked this vigorously after we got married. You decide on the lifestyle, identify what you need to do to get it, how you must live, and your obstacles, and then knock them down one by one. I knew exactly how much we owed and only paid expenses by check so we could track every single penny. I knew what percent of interest each debt charged and ranked them so the highest-interest debts were paid off first. It did not take very long until we were debt free, because I had a specific goal, developed a detailed plan with clear deadlines and reward milestones attached, then took action. On this journey to being debt-free, we certainly faced some tough challenges, but my wife and I persevered and eventually broke one more chain that was slowing us down – the chain of bad debt. It was as if we just spiked our engine with nitrous oxide. The RPMs surged because we both felt better and more confident and now we could invest our money elsewhere.

Take the time to analyze in great detail your personal financial position. *Self-discipline* is critical as is making sure that everyone on the family team is in line with the goal and plan. Once you know where you are starting from, moving forward in a deliberate manner is much easier and more productive.

- How much money do you have coming in and how much do you pay out to live <u>modestly</u>?

- Stop paying for things with cash because once you break that $100 bill, it quickly gets spent and it's tough to remember where every penny went.

- Only pay for things using checks or a credit card, assuming you pay off the credit card every month.

- How much debt do you owe and to whom?

- What are the exact interest rates? Rate them from highest to lowest and pay off the highest ones first.

- When you are living modestly, how much extra is left over to pay toward bad debt?

3. What kind of **gear** are you packing? Do you have a map, a cell phone, DVD and CD players, or are you still using an 8-track? Will you be traveling light until you get some

momentum or is it better for you to over-pack and travel more slowly? What about sightseeing along the way? Is your journey going to be all work and no play, or will you have lots of fun along the way?

What you bring on your life's journey will make the difference between being happy or miserable. Money is a tool to use wisely, not squirrel away somewhere because you are afraid to spend it. Your map is your resource confirming exactly how other people made this same journey. From Chicago to Denver you would not want to take Interstate 94 headed east, would you? You could still eventually make it to Denver but I would not want to circumnavigate the globe. With books, CDs, DVDs, and any other resource you can find that shows HOW to make the trip without getting lost, you are assured to have an already-traveled map, which makes reaching your destination just a matter of time. What to pack will come from both your and other people's experiences.

By answering these three questions you have taken your personal inventory, but the most important thing is that you just get started. Get some miles on those tires. Once a body is in motion, it will stay in motion and gradually pick up momentum unless something is allowed to slow it down or stop it. Warm up and prepare your vehicle, keep your tank as full as possible, pack for the ride of your life, and then get moving right away!

4.2   Get the tissues, here comes the sob story

Where was I when I started? The better you understand where I began and what I went through, the more you will be willing to apply in your life what I am teaching right now. You will see that I am no different than you, that success is not a mystery but a repeatable, methodical formula thus you will believe you can do it too. The only difference between you and me is that I started on my lifestyle quest many years ago. I applied the success tools in this book, just as I am suggesting you do, and they worked well for me. You need to first decide on your destination and develop the right mindset, next take your personal inventory, and now you are ready to begin.

I left off telling you how I stalked successful people on the streets of Duluth. The information I was able to gather made a lot of sense to me, which motivated me to begin to search for an "opportunity." I started with the local daily newspaper and found it had a "Business Opportunities" section, so I scoured it eagerly, looking for anything that would catch my eye. It did not take long to find what I thought was just the right opportunity. The ad said I could make $100,000 a year with no experience and they were willing to train me completely. This sounded perfect – I loved the money, and I really had no experience, so if they wanted to train me I was in! I called the number and was connected with one heck of a salesman working for Bankline America.

He was smart and he gave me a wonderful pitch. To this day, I still remember the conversation that took place in July 1989. He took the time to study me and asked numerous skillful fact-finding questions. How old was I? Where did I live? Was I going to college? Why did I call them? What was I looking for? How hard was I willing to work? This went on for more than an hour, but I was so excited I felt like it was only a few minutes. He did the *take-away* close on me and hung up leaving me hanging on the idea of, "If we are interested in you, I will call YOU back." I hoped and prayed he did. I was an easy sell. I was hungry, naïve, and desperate. He had me hook, line, and sinker. Oh, if only I had a trusted business coach THEN, who could have helped me understand what was going on. I had been sold by a pro but he used this powerful skill to rip people off and I was about to be the next body for him to shoot down.

When he called back the next day, he gave me the scoop. I was to send his company a cashier's check for $3,300.00 using FedEx next day. My heart sank. I did not pay attention to much of anything after he said THREE THOUSAND, THREE HUNDRED DOLLARS. I do remember a little, though. He explained that the money paid for my starting printed supplies and gave me my own "legal territory" in which only I could make the money. I would set up credit card displays in all of the local businesses, and when someone filled out the secured-credit-card application and mailed it along with the $49.95 fee, I would get paid back $14 of the $49.95. Credit cards were not nearly as easy to obtain in the late 80s as they are now, so many people were willing to apply for and use a credit card secured by monies they had in savings with the bank that issued the credit card. It was a great opportunity for them to get a credit card, build their credit rating, or rebuild if they had messed it up. This all sounded great to me except for the THIRTY THREE HUNDRED DOLLARS. I felt like this was my only shot. He wisely gave me a deadline and implied a lot of interest from other prospective people who wanted in and of course, FIRST COME FIRST SERVED! I thought, "This is it Allen, you snooze you lose, and I don't lose!"

The problem was that I did not have that kind of money. I could not even afford to live on campus. I had a little more than $300 in my savings account and this was my nest egg saved up from the nickels and dimes I got for waiting on tables. I believed it takes money to make money, so my $300 was committed – no question. But I still needed $3,000 more. I did NOT have any immediate family I could go to for that kind of money, so I called the only person I thought would be willing to help if she could, my grandmother.

She lived alone, and many years later I learned, just survived on Social Security of about $650 per month and a pension of close to $50 per month from the factory where she had worked for more than 20 years. She told me she had managed to save up a grand total of a little more than $6,000 for her retirement and that was her only nest egg. I begged and pleaded and finally got her to send me $3,000 of her retirement money. These numbers may not sound like much to some people, but really sit down and let it sink in. She had nothing, but she believed in me and I had allowed myself to believe in a snake. I got the money together and sent it out next day and hoped I was the first person with their money in. As luck would have it I was. WOW! Lucky me.

Within a few days of my 19th birthday I received a box from Bankline. It contained 200 cardboard credit card displays that I needed to fold into position and stuff with the 7,500 applications. I was ecstatic. This was my big break and I was going to seize it. The only transportation I had at the time was a 1977 650 Kawasaki motorcycle that I bought from my uncle a month prior. I drove to Goodwill and bought a maroon briefcase because I was a businessman now. I loaded it with supplies and a college-ruled composition notebook, just like the one I used in my gum business. Then I headed out to talk to the local business people to get their permission to put up my displays in their stores.

I went to many places and asked but was told NO, their counter space is too precious and I would not be allowed to put anything there unless I paid THEM rent for the space. The display was only about three inches by four inches and stood nine inches tall. I felt like I was banging my head against a wall but what choice did I have? I had to keep moving. Sales is a numbers game. Ask enough people to buy and you will eventually make your first sale. Finally, I got one to agree, and then two, and as a result I developed a pitch that worked and went back to the same people who had said no in the beginning and many changed their minds. Within a week or so, there were Bankline America displays in almost EVERY convenience store, gas station, Laundromat, bar, restaurant, and gym I could find in Duluth, Hermantown, Two

Harbors and Cloquet, Minnesota and Superior, Wisconsin. I was set up and ready to get rich.

Every few days I drove to each display and restocked the missing applications and excitedly waited for my big check to arrive. I had a detailed route to maximize my drive time and use the least gas as well as a log of every display and application stocked in that display. I was organized and ready to make a killing. I kept this whole process up for a couple more weeks when in early August I got my first check in the mail. I was so excited to open the envelope that I practically tore it into pieces. When I looked at it, I could not believe my eyes. It was written for $98! Ninety-eight lousy dollars? This had to be some kind of mistake so I called the company and they confirmed only seven of the thousands of applications I put out there had been sent in. To say my heart sank a bit would be an understatement. However, I am not easily discouraged and believed the next check would be better. In mid-August my second check arrived and that was for $182. A grand total of 20 applications have been sent in from which I earned a total of $280. More than 7,000 applications had been taken out of my displays but only 20 had been sent in – this did not make any sense. I foolishly had put myself in a position in which I was unable to track my own income. How did I really know only 20 applications had been filled out and sent in? Maybe 1,000 had but perhaps the company just decided not to pay me. How could I know for sure since I had no way to accurately track and verify production?

Because I was almost out of applications, I called in to order more and to my absolute shock the number for Bankline America was no longer in service. I thought I must have made a mistake so I called again and again, not wanting to believe my ears, but I got the same recording saying the number was no longer in service. I did not know what to do so I asked around and was advised to call the Attorney General's office for the state of Texas, where the company was based. What I learned on that call opened my eyes to the harshness of the real business world like nothing before. I learned that this company had done this to thousands of people across the country. People who paid the same amount of money as I had now had nothing to show for it. The $182 check bounced, so all I had to show for all my efforts was $98. I was in a worse position than ever, when you considered that my savings were gone AND I owed my grandmother $3,000, still did not own a car, and had no idea what I was going to do next. The moment I thought everything was going my way, life just knocked me down in the dirt yet again. Little did I know at the time, when it rains it sometimes pours.

4.3   What - there's more?

Two days after all of this unfolded, I was walking across Superior Street in Duluth to mail the insurance check for my motorcycle and WHAM, I got hit by a car. I bounced off of one car, ended up in the oncoming lane and another car narrowly missed me. My girlfriend Debbie was walking into the gas station as I was hit and saw the whole thing. I got up, was in shock, and waved the car that hit me to go ahead because I was fine. Then I walked to the mailbox on the corner, pulled down the lid with my left arm and when I tried to raise my right arm to put in the envelope, nothing happened. My arm just swung limp as a noodle so I grabbed the envelope with my left hand and stuffed it in the slot. The lady who hit me had pulled over and was frantic, I was still in shock. Debbie ran over and the woman offered to drive us to the hospital. I knew something was very wrong but told her I was OK. She insisted and so the three of us drove to St. Luke's emergency room.

We got there and the doctor immediately knew something was very wrong. My right arm hung about six inches lower than it should have and my collar bone was pointing upward. He told me I had a third-degree separation, which really meant nothing to me, but right about then the pain started to kick in. He told me I would need surgery and may never be able to use my right arm the same way again. Here I am, a 19-year-old college dropout with no money, no family to fall back on, I had just been conned out of $3,300, and then was hit by a car. I have learned since then that when life seems the absolute darkest it is testing you, pushing you further than your perceived limits just to see how you will answer the call. Will you give up or will you fight? Will your character survive or will your spirit be broken? These are without a doubt the times when you must tighten your boots, grab on firmly to something, and hold on for dear life until the bumpy ride is over. I later learned after getting knocked down multiple times and getting back up to face life again, that it is these times that have always preceded my greatest victories.

Surgery was scheduled for the next week and I was scared, to say the least. I was alone, injured, penniless, and afraid of needles. I had never had surgery before and was totally petrified by the thought of being knocked out, cut open, and screwed back together. But I showed up, got my IV, and before I knew it the whole procedure was over. However, I will never forget that day. Certain moments in life either make us or break us and whatever occurs is because of the level of heart we possess. When I woke up from surgery there was ONLY one person there to greet me with a smile, only ONE. It was Debbie, who had stuck with me every day since the accident, Debbie alone who stood there with a balloon, a rose, and a card. The entire time following the surgery, I never got a single card or phone call from family. It was more confirmation of how alone I was on this journey. I believe God puts certain people in our lives for certain reasons and it is up to us to learn *why* and *how* to benefit from our relationships with these people. As I have said, some are to be examples of what is right, how we should act and think, while others are warning signs of what not to do. Some are harder to notice while others are like bright neon signs saying, "Beware! Bridge Out Ahead." Debbie was put into my life only a few months prior to the accident as a friend and companion, but that day of my surgery I knew deep down that she was also my life partner. She was the single greatest gift I had ever been given.

As I recovered, I faced an ever-increasing problem; I had next to no money and now could not work in my only available J.O.B. I could not bus tables nor wait on them with only one arm. My right arm was taped to my side for the next six weeks. I did not have the luxury of taking pain pills and lying around as I healed. I had to continue to survive. I was able to talk my frat brothers into covering my house expenses until I was able to recover and get back to work. Then I would pay them back. I attempted to get Plush Pippin to find a different job for me but was unsuccessful. However, after closing a door, life did open a window for me at my second J.O.B. I went to the manager, Pete, told him what had happened to me and asked for his help. I have wanted to be able to say thanks to Grandma's Sports Garden ever since in a very public way, and this book finally gives me that opportunity. Pete could have turned me down like Plush Pippin but, instead, he gave me the task of taking cover charges at the door and assisting the bouncers any way I could with one arm. It was only on weekends and was not much money, but it ended up being enough to survive as I healed and got stronger.

By late September I was so low on money I was not able to buy food from the grocery store, so what I did was get creative. At Plush Pippin they would offer the pies that did not sell to the employees for only $1 before throwing them in the trash. For the next month I lived on pie. I would buy them for $1 and could live on one or two each day. By mid-October I was able to start working as a waiter again. I took every shift I could get at both J.O.B.s and quickly repaid my frat brothers every penny I owed them. This brings me to November of 1989, the single most life-changing month of my life.

4.4   Life finally pays off

I may have been broke, but I kept my word. I was in a doctor's office for a check on my shoulder and happened upon a magazine put out by the National Fire Protection Association. In this journal was information that changed my life, even though at the time it was just another thing to read while passing the time. I proceeded to learn that more than 5,000 people die in fires every year, that almost all of the deaths occurred in the home, and that most homes were not prepared to deal with fire. This was just like when Brian offered to buy the first piece of gum from me in junior high. An idea popped into my head: I could save people's lives for a living by selling safety equipment.

I had no idea what to do, what items to sell, how to get into their homes to present my products, or much of anything else, **but I had an idea** and was excited about it. I began to talk to firefighters and ask very simple questions, such as:

"Why do so many people die in their homes?"

"Why don't people have the protection they need?"

"What does a house need to be prepared for a fire?"

I asked many more questions and did quite a bit of research into other safety equipment sales companies, as to how and what they sold. I was looking for successful patterns to mimic. I became convinced there was a huge money-making opportunity for me by selling safety equipment door-to-door. I was not scared of door-to-door sales because I had done that so many times before for Boy Scouts and school fundraisers. I was willing to talk to people, so I went right to work. What I did was really simple. I took a piece of paper and typed up my first Home Fire Safety

Survey. I came up with my business name, drew a logo and made hundreds of white and yellow copies. I put a piece of carbon paper in the middle, stapled them together, put this survey on my clipboard and went to work.

Beginning on November 20th 1989, I went all around my neighborhood and knocked on doors telling people I was there to discuss fire safety. Some let me in but most just slammed the door in my face. I proceeded to teach them what I had learned about fire safety, about how they will have a fire someday and should prepare now before the fire happens, and ended with attempting to sell them my safety equipment. However, the real challenge was that I did not yet have any safety equipment. I was testing the waters and as a result learned what I was doing really could work. So when I made a sale and took their check I immediately had to find a source for my products. Gradually I read more books on sales, did hundreds of demonstrations, and developed my communication (sales) skills, and I made thousands of dollars in sales in a single week. **This process took me about three months of trial and error, ups and downs, but I never lost confidence in myself after making my first sale.** I knew I would succeed because I made more money from it than I did in an entire eight-hour shift in the restaurant. This was my starting point!

I never ended up complaining to any governmental agency about Bankline America because I accepted personal accountability for my mistakes and wanted to move on. I knew whining would neither pay the rent, nor was the government really going to get my money back. Next time, I would not be so easily blinded by my own excitement and greed (Emotional Discipline) or put myself in a position in which I was completely at the mercy of any company to accurately track my income (Financial Intelligence). I stood up, learned, and went on because I believed there was not enough time for a self-pity stop on my journey. I decided to let it go and move forward, instead of allowing this experience to remain a negative mental weight pulling me down forever (Leadership). People will wrong you in life but in order to live your ideal lifestyle, you must let it go so it has no more power over you. If it's criminal then report it to the police, but if it's anything else, just move on because you have no time to waste. Karma is a beautiful thing; we all get back 10-fold in life what we give out.

On that November day in 1989, I traded in my old clunker vehicle of a J.O.B. for a new faster vehicle called sales and the resulting ownership of my own productivity. That was the day I stopped working for someone else and went to work developing myself. By not giving up, learning how to sell, and staying focused upon the prize, I earned my financial freedom 13 years later. I would never again trade my hours for dollars, rent my life away for a few scraps given by my employer. As of that November day in 1989, I controlled my own destiny because I controlled my productivity (time, emotional energy, and experience). Instead of selling it to someone else, my productivity was focused completely upon achieving my ideal lifestyle. Because I was now using the right vehicle for me, I began to pick up speed and momentum as the miles passed by faster and faster. It took me until late 1990 but I paid my grandmother back every penny I borrowed from her plus interest.

The present is all that really matters. Live in the present. Take out the mental trash, whatever is keeping you from this moment, and focus on the HERE and NOW. The ONLY thing we have any real power over is right NOW, because we have the power to make choices. What we choose to think and do in the NOW becomes the direction we are traveling in. Our choices shape our future and who we will eventually become. One of the most important choices we can ever make is WHOM we allow to travel with us.

4.5   Truth # 4 Action Points

You know where you are headed and are passionately focused upon getting there. You are excited, feel the need for speed, and want to get going. You understand life will throw many obstacles in the road, which you will need to overcome to achieve what you want. From time to time, you may even need to take a detour, but you don't want to get lost so you must be confident of your origination point and roadmap. To travel as fast as possible in the correct direction, you must first determine your starting point. How?

A.   <u>Decide which type of vehicle you will use to get to your desired destination</u>. How do you currently make your money? Is your financial vehicle fast or slow? Do you control it or are you controlled by it? Is your productivity making someone else rich while you remain broke? If you are not currently using the best vehicle for your trip, then you must set in motion a plan to trade in the old and replace it with the new. Ownership and effective direction of your own time, emotional energy, and experience toward obtaining the way of life you desire, are critical to making the journey a successful one.

B.   <u>Know your current financial starting point exactly</u>. In order to point your financial vehicle in the right direction and be sure it runs efficiently, you must first know your starting point by completing an accurate and current personal financial statement – a picture of how your money flows in and out. Your personal inventory must include your income statement, balance sheet, and determine your net worth. To complete your ideal lifestyle journey, you must direct and manage your financial vehicle effectively! You have got to know how much fuel you are starting with in your tank, become aware of any money leaks so you can take steps to plug them, and be sure of how you will refill along the way so you don't run out of gas. If you are unaware of how to complete a personal financial statement, seek the assistance of a professional accountant.

C. <u>Pack appropriately and get started</u>. Gather together every resource you have at your access to help guide you on this trip. These resources can be books, CDs, notes you have taken or people you trust to guide you along the way. In order to make the journey, we all need an accurate map or we will just wander aimlessly, hoping to succeed. The accuracy of the information sources you pack will determine how quickly you make the trip and how comfortable you will be along the way. There will be some unavoidable bumps in the road, so the better prepared you are, the less you will be affected.

TRUTH # 5

Where you will end up,
depends a lot upon who travels with you.

Great spirits have always encountered opposition from mediocre
minds. *The mediocre mind is incapable of understanding the man*
who refuses to bow blindly to conventional prejudices and chooses
instead to express his opinions courageously and honestly.
-Albert Einstein, quoted in New York Times, March 13, 1940.

5.1   The right environment

At about the age of 11, I was at a family Christmas gathering.
Being the oldest grandchild, I was often asked what I wanted to
be when I grew up. When the question came that year, I was
prepared. I said, "I will be a millionaire before I am 30 and after
that I do not know what I want to do." Here I was a little kid
with my chest puffed out feeling all proud of myself because I
KNEW what I was going to be but the reaction I received was
not what I expected. There was silence and eventually laughter. I

was crushed and slinked out of the room to be alone. I eventually became angry and developed an "I'll show them" attitude, which in a way was good, but as I already told you too, negative emotions will only give you emotional juice for a limited time. On this day, I became mentally clearer – I was hurt and I needed to separate myself from the people who hurt me. As soon as I was able, I needed to leave. I loved these people but they simply thought differently than I did.

Here is how I look at it now with a much clearer emotionally-neutral mind. I understand now why they laughed. Nobody in our family had ever done what I said I was going to do. How could they believe in a child who had no track record? After all, it is human nature to immediately be suspicious of or even reject the unfamiliar – new ideas are scary to some people. This is why I had to separate myself from these people and climb into my vehicle alone. This is why I moved to Duluth at age 18 to begin. Are you passionate enough about your dreams to do the same? Are you willing to go it alone temporarily? This was a necessity for me. To have stayed around my Winona circle of influence would have been my dream's death sentence. It would have resulted in me getting a local J.O.B. and repeating many of the same patterns of struggle I had seen and still do. This was absolutely NOT acceptable for me. I felt like it was me against the world, but I had decided the world was not going to win!!!

Lifestyle *(my definition)*

A person's way of life resulting from the <u>decisions</u> they made – good or bad.

I strive for the easiest understanding I can find for complex subjects. I often find that the more complicated something appears, the more likely it is that there is someone behind the scenes trying to overcomplicate matters in order to confuse people. Every day we make choices, large and small. It is these decisions that when added up determine the lifestyle we live. When we decide poorly, we end up fat, alone, broke, or in jail. But when we make good choices over the long haul, we are able to enjoy life and live at whatever level we decide upon.

An early example of a winner for me was my uncle Bernie. He was my godfather, and I put him on a pedestal. As a teenager, I looked up to him because he owned a very successful business building farm silos, had a beautiful wife and two little girls, and had set a high school sit-up record of 1,000 sit-ups without stopping. He seemed to have the world in the palms of his hands. He was someone I wanted to be just like when I grew up and I loved the weeks I got to work for him before going to college. But that all changed. Bernie started to drink heavily as he got older and life's pressures grew. Gradually his business fell apart as did his marriage and his relationship with his daughters. Bernie was working with my cousin Mark, who at 32 was a married father of three and self-employed fixing silos. On June 27, 2005, Mark and Bernie, then 50, died in a 60-foot fall from a silo they were fixing.

Bernie chose to drink. He chose his companions and how he invested his time, emotional energy, and experience. He chose to throw away the reputation and loving relationships he had worked so hard to build. He chose to reject all of the outside help that was offered to him. He chose to go from being an example to follow to being a warning sign. When he died, he left a lot of hurt people, unfulfilled dreams and missed opportunities. He also left me wondering why and how a man I had loved and respected so much, who had it all in my eyes, would be willing to throw it away. Unfortunately, many members of my family have allowed addiction to be their demise. I decided very early on that I may not be able to change my genetics, but I CAN choose what to be addicted to!

I chose to become addicted to the passionate pursuit of enjoying my ideal lifestyle. I am addicted to being the best person I can be and making my life an adventure worth living, so that one day I would be able to help other people to break free from what they had allowed to hold them down. I often think about what someone would write in a biography about how I spent my *dash* between birth and death. When they write yours, will it match what you desired your life to be?

5.2   A crab in the bucket

We make choices based upon the information available to us at the moment. The more accurate the source of the information, the better the choices we end up making. Where do we get most of our information?

We get it from the people we surround ourselves with. So many want the lifestyle of the rich and successful, but continue to hang around with other people struggling to pay their rent and wonder **why** they never seem to break free from the cycle of existing paycheck to paycheck. If you want to learn how to fix your car, are you going to ask a plumber or a mechanic? Will you ask your lawyer how to fix your shoulder pain, or will you go to a doctor? Both of these answers seem obvious, so, I have one more question for you. When you yearn to earn $100,000 per year, whom are you going to ask?

Find other people who have what you want and mimic them. You will gradually become just like those whom you hang around. If you continue to lie with dogs, don't be surprised when you wake up with fleas. Or put another way, misery loves company. Why are there so many sayings about the same thing? Maybe it's because their message is TRUE. Remember, start with the truth because you will eventually end with it. This is why I named this truth, "Where you end up, depends a lot upon who travels with you."

My objective is to help as many people as I can be Anti-Sheepitized and break free from the herd, to help them to stop being *normal*. The normal or average American earns only $26,036 per year and maintains an average debt load of $18,700 not including a home mortgage. Normal people blame other people for their problems when they ought to just look in the mirror. Normal people exist broke in spirit wandering from birth to death weighted down by regrets, as if they are wearing shoes made out of lead. Why in the world would you want to be normal? I choose instead to be an abnormal person because I want an *abnormal* lifestyle. I seek to align myself with other abnormal people. I avoid, like the plague, those normal people who seem to have made it their mission to discourage other people motivated to improve themselves.

Normal people believe the only right path to success is the one they are on. I ask them, "How is that path really working for you? When you are lost do you just drive faster and attempt to bring other people into your car to be lost with you, so you don't have to suffer your situation alone?" Judge people by their results, NOT their words, because talk is cheap. Is the person giving you marital advice on his or her third marriage? Is someone telling you that you MUST have a college degree in order to make it in this world, even though they don't have one, or have done nothing with theirs? I chose not to use a piece of paper from a college to attempt to prove how smart I was. I chose to let my results speak for me.

I have seen small-minded people like these discourage others with so much potential thousands of times over the years. I believe most people just need someone to believe in them and say kind words of encouragement. What does this cost? It takes the same effort to build someone up as it does to break them down, so why do so many choose to continue breaking others down? Any idiot with a match can burn down a house but it takes someone special to be able to build one. What kind of person will you choose to be, an arsonist or a carpenter?

Imagine for a moment you are treading water in the ocean of success. All you have to do is keep you head above water long enough and you will get everything you ever desired. EVERY single limiting person you continue to allow to stay in your life is like adding a five-pound weight to your ankle. Add one and you can still tread with little additional effort. But add two or three or even more and gradually even the strongest of swimmers will get pulled under and drown. Every person in your life is either helping you or hurting you – nobody is in the middle. As long as you allow negative, small-minded, or limiting people into your vehicle, not only will it be a miserable trip, but every time you attempt to get onto the Path of Performance, they will shoot you down. Why would you expect anything different from them? Insecure, small-minded idiots with matches are very dangerous.

You must carefully select the source of the information seeds you allow to be planted in your mental field. Whatever is allowed to get in will grow, good or bad. I find the suspicious nature of all these small-minded, fearful people very interesting. When you think about it, the path to an amazing lifestyle should look unfamiliar to these people. They have not done anything extraordinary with their lives. The following example may explain why.

When fishing for crabs, you only need to keep a lid on the bucket to contain the first crab. When you add a second crab to the bucket, the lid is no longer necessary because neither crab will allow the other to escape. This is natural mediocrity at work! When one crab tries to get out, the other one just grabs onto it and pulls it right back in. A third crab even makes this process easier because now you have two to pull down the wannabe escapee. This is the "herd" mentality. This is how sheeple think. They think they are helping each other by planting weeds of fear into each other's fields, which kill every good seed sown of prosperity. It is much easier to suffer when you have a buddy to do it with. It lends validity to blaming others for your lack of success. When both of you blame "the man," then it MUST be true. All this kind of thinking leads to is ending up on some person's plate, in a nice restaurant, as a wonderfully prepared crab cake. Open up your mind, embrace new ideas, and welcome things that are different. We do not experience personal growth within our comfort zone. Support those around you who are attempting to break free because what goes around comes around. The people you emotionally support today may be the same ones who help you later in life. To keep others down is foolish, because everyone loses.

My final point on this is at my current place in life, I have chosen to go full circle and work very hard at reestablishing relationships with good people I once believed held me back. I understand people and their motivations so much better now. Life is enriched by fruitful relationships. Mutually beneficial relationships are what make life such a beautiful thing. Don't attempt to crush my dreams. Help me, and I will in turn do whatever I can to help you. Building new bridges with these people AFTER you have clearly established yourself within your vehicle and on your own road to ideal lifestyle achievement, will hopefully do for you what it has for me and make you feel whole. Now I know that none of these people will be able to drag me down, because first, I won't let them and second, few will ever even try to say negative things around me because I have proven my ability to back up my words with actions. I have built a solid reputation and many have begun to ask for my input on challenges they encounter.

How can I truly be of value to those I love if I am not true to myself? I had to discover what I needed in order to enjoy my ideal lifestyle. The point is that I had to discover who I really was. This meant I had to drive my own vehicle alone at times, focusing upon constant self-improvement, and doing my best to be honest with myself. Now I am a husband and father and I have an obligation to be there for my wife and my sons. I have a duty to create an environment within our home that nurtures positive personal growth so all of us can continue to grow and become the best we can be. How can I effectively do this if I am not true to myself?

5.3 Who are you taking along for the ride & where will they sit?

You are the driver and therefore control who can get in and how far they may travel with you. I believe that if you want to see your future, all you have to do is look at the people you have surrounded yourself with. When we choose people who add to our lives, we have chosen wisely. This results in a full gas tank, a charged battery, and an accurate road map. If we chose poorly, at best we are slowed down and at worst we never complete our journey.

I have made good and bad choices about people. Initially I simply did not have the expertise to choose wisely, to know what to look for, and who to avoid. I was easily fooled because I wanted to believe the best in everyone and this led to being misled and taken advantage of often. Each time I got back up, learned from the experience, and went on. I rarely if ever give people second chances. I believe very much in the adage, "Fool me once, shame on you. Fool me twice, shame on ME." I have built numerous teams of people who increase my emotional energy, provide me with much more time to do as I wish, are accurate sources of knowledge, hold me accountable for implementation, challenge me by being an example for me to follow, and ultimately help me to continue to enjoy the lifestyle of my dreams. Good people in the proper places on your life teams are worth their weight in gold.

Success is all about keeping your moving vehicle between the lines on the road, making more good decisions than bad. One of the most significant things I ever learned was that *success is a team sport*. Contrary to this, I was raised with the belief that in order for something to be done right, I had to do it myself. That is NOT how successful people think. We all have those things we are naturally gifted at doing and we must put ourselves in positions in which we can be rewarded for doing those things. Play to your strengths and hire other people to assist with your weaknesses. I am not referring to learning a new skill like golf or speaking Spanish. Talents or strengths are our brain's hardware and skills are like the software. I am neither naturally gifted at bookkeeping nor do I even like doing the work. However it still needs to be done, so I hire someone else who is naturally a good bookkeeper, even though bookkeeping is a skill I could acquire if I had to.

5.4   Choosing Teams

I have decided that in order to enjoy the lifestyle of my dreams, I need to build three teams of people. I am constantly adding new good people and getting rid of those who no longer are a good fit.

1. <u>Emotional Support Team (EST)</u>.
   These people ride in your vehicle because you want to keep them very close. They are there for you when you are down, not because they enjoy seeing someone else suffer, but because they want to help. They will stroke your ego when needed and tell you everything will be OK. They are the people you can call at 2 a.m. just to talk. These are the GOOD people you allow into your emotional zone, and it can be scary if you allow the wrong ones in. These people have emotional power to affect you because you let them. Choose carefully!

   They can include family, friends, even your dog. If you

want a friend in business, buy a dog and put it on this team. These people (and animals) make you FEEL better by being around you. They don't just allow you to sit there and cry on their shoulders. They listen but also help you to get back in the saddle to ride again as quickly as possible. You will seek to please these people and push even harder because you won't want to let them down. These people add to you and increase your emotional energy, because they give you more juice to push even harder. They do not drag you down, cause you to question the pursuit of what is important to you, or try to limit you in any non-destructive action.

2. <u>Peak Performance Team (PPT).</u>
These people may climb into my vehicle for short periods of time. Many of them work with other clients as well and have their own productive financial vehicles to drive. They drive alongside me, in a convoy of vehicles driving down the road of success. Just like the name implies, these people or groups are there to help me perform at the highest level possible. Life only pays on results, so I seek out the absolute best coaches and teachers possible. I want people who challenge my current physical, mental, and spiritual self in order to help me stretch my mind so I may achieve at an even higher level.

There can be some crossover between EST and PPT in the case of a business coach or personal trainer. They help me improve and are there to boost my emotional energy. When I first began my journey I had no clue as to the value these kinds of people would bring. As I grew wiser, I sought out the best team members money could buy. Advice is usually worth what you pay for it, and free advice is often worthless. This is your <u>life</u> we are talking about and you NEED the best information in order to make the smartest decisions and be the most productive. I have often heard that knowledge is power but I disagree with this notion. Only *applied* knowledge is power. To know something is good, but it is not good enough. Accurate knowledge is to your future what light is to a dark room because you must be able to see where you are going. Find an accurate source of the specific knowledge you need and remain willing to keep your source accountable for results as well.

Very Important – I do my best to keep this in mind, specifically with this team. I hired them to help me perform at a certain level. They are strictly on the team to produce and if they don't produce, they get cut from the team! This can be very tough because you form emotional bonds with people who are with you during especially tough times, but business is business. If my lawyer does not produce when I need him to, then I will seek out a new one. To not do so would jeopardize my entire lifestyle journey. When filling spots on your PPT, follow this simple rule: *Hire slowly and fire fast!*

Some examples of past and present people (organizations) on my PPT:

- Business Coach
- Life Coach
- Entrepreneurs' Organization
- Law Firm
- Accounting Firm
- Real Estate Agent
- Financial Planner
- Key staff in my companies
- Personal Trainer
- Golf Coach
- Sailing Coach
- Nutritionist

3.   <u>Task-Doer Team (TDT).</u>
This could also be called my *Quality of Life* or *Service Team*. These people don't ride in my vehicle much. I pick

them up, they do their jobs, and I drop them off. My time and emotional energy are precious to me. Therefore I choose not to spend either of them doing things I don't like. Instead, I hire someone else to do the tasks that I either cannot do or am unwilling to do.

Here is an example of what I mean. In 1992 when I was living in southern California, I was ironing my dress shirts one night. I had always loathed this task. I had to spot treat, wash, iron, and starch them just so I could look professional each day. I suddenly got the idea to time myself and see just how long this whole process took me. Each shirt took 20 minutes. Then I called a dry cleaner and asked how much they charge to do the same process and learned something that changed my way of thinking forever. They charged $2 per shirt and I could only do three shirts per hour, therefore I was saving, or paying myself depending upon how you think, only $6 per hour to do something I could not stand. Then I calculated how much money I would have made if I had spent that same one hour doing what I do best in my business, and the contrast of intelligently investing my time and emotional energy versus trying to SAVE money was clear. I was losing money doing something I hated. Other than in an emergency situation, I have never ironed a shirt again. Since then I applied this same way of thinking to mowing the lawn, shoveling the snow, and cleaning my house, along with numerous other tasks. I do what I enjoy and what pays me well. Then I hire someone else to do everything else!

Because of my decision to become great at one thing that pays me well, I can enjoy my life doing things that make me and those on my EST happy. As a result, my time and emotional energy are freed up to invest as I choose. Instead of ironing my own shirts, I will go to my son's sporting event. Instead of getting frustrated fixing my own car, I am able to read a business book or watch a movie with my wife. Freedom to choose is the lifestyle I have chosen.

I emphasize the same point with your TDT as I did with your PPT. When my TDT members do not produce, I replace them right away. This can be tough to do with someone who has been working for you over a long period of time, but if the task is not being done correctly then you must replace a team member. These people are hired to do a task, so get what you paid for and remain *emotionally neutral*.

The most important thing money buys you is time. If a normal person retires at age 65 but you do so at 35 because you took ownership of your personal productivity at a young age, then money bought you 30 years! For 30 more years, you will get to spend your time exactly as you choose AND have the money necessary to enjoy whatever you choose. Find something you enjoy from which you can get paid, take ownership of your own productivity (time, emotional energy, and experience), and then pay others to do everything else that distracts you from your ideal lifestyle pursuit.

Some examples of past and present people on my TDT:

• Mechanic	• Masseuse
• Landscaper	• Stylist
• Car Detailer	• Construction Manager
• House Cleaner	• Nanny
• Drycleaner	• Handyman

5.5   My key team members

There are always certain people who play a greater role in our lives than others will, and for me there are really three. I decided to put this part into the book to show you not just who they are and why they have been so important, but how I deliberately worked to develop the relationships.

1. **My wife, Debbie.** She is my lifestyle journey co-pilot. She sits in the passenger's seat of my vehicle. She is the ONLY one who ever gets to ride shotgun. Going all the way back to the time in the hospital after the car hit me, I knew there was something very special about her. We dated for five years and have been married since 1994. A climber does not just fall on top of a mountain, nor did our relationship build itself.

    During my never-ending study of what it takes to become and remain a winner, I came across a book called The *Millionaire Mind,* which really affected me. It's a book dedicated to the study of self-made millionaires from all walks of life. I found it fascinating that 25 percent of the whole project, seemed to be focused upon finding the right spouse. Now if a book that studied thousands of winners who *made it* spends one-fourth of its content on spouse selection and maintenance, I have to believe this is a very important topic. I found it amazing how much of what was in that book Debbie and I have already been doing by working together over a long period of time to build our life together.

    Here are some specifics that have helped us create a marriage that has stood the test of time.

    A. <u>Clear Vision.</u> Before getting married, I came up with the image to the right to explain to my wife what being married meant to me. The big circle in the center represents "us" and our life together. The smaller black circle on the left is "my" life and the equal-sized black circle on the right is "hers." After having two children, I added the smaller grey circles at the bottom.

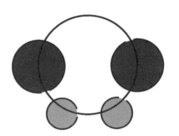

We share a life, which is bigger than all of the other circles, because if that one is not healthy then everyone in our family will suffer. When we married, I was concerned that my wife would try to settle me down, change me, or get in the way of accomplishing my other life objectives. I have seen this occur in many other marriages and they eventually fell apart or the two people grew to be unhappy but were unwilling to do anything to change their situation.

I decided to skydive, be an entrepreneur, learn to sail, move all over the country, and much more. And Debbie decided to earn a master's degree in marketing, become a third-degree black belt in tae kwon do, and develop her body like that of a female bodybuilder. We SHARE a life but still respect each other's need to achieve our own personal dreams as well. Only when our individual lives begin to negatively affect OUR shared life together, do we make changes. This way we can be true to who we are, feel fulfilled and not controlled, and still be able to build a strong, healthy relationship together. By having this vision and understanding, we have avoided many hurt feelings, resentments, and potential marriage-killing issues.

B. <u>Open and honest Communication.</u> It does not matter whether we are discussing our dreams in life or the current balance in the checkbook. We openly talk about everything under the sun. This sounds easy but it is really tough sometimes, especially if you need to tell the other person there is something wrong. We strive not to control each other. I believe my idea to treat our household as a business has helped. We have regular family board meetings and attempt to approach things in as logical (emotionally neutral) a fashion as possible. In all partnerships there still must be a decision maker and leader. I don't buy into the concept of a 50/50 relationship. This does not imply either of us attempts to control the other, but there is a clear 51/49 when a key decision needs to be made.

It sure helps when you have a family vision and mission statement. When you have the foundation laid and a good idea of where your relationship is headed, then it becomes easier to be and remain thoughtful, caring, loving, respectful, and appreciative. When it really boils down to the essence – we really WANT to be together and share this adventure of a life. We have therefore decided to learn and do whatever is necessary to achieve our objective because WE are a team.

C. <u>Conflict Resolution.</u> We never go to bed angry. We know people who will go days without talking when they are having a big fight. How destructive is a lack of communication? We promised very early in our relationship to stay up as late as necessary in order to "work it out." We both have worked very hard to develop healthy communication skills so the other person feels valued and important, so discussions are not about winning when we have conflict. We have our share of *spirited discussions*, but I believe it is how you deal with conflict that is important. Too many times I have heard of marriages breaking up and the couple says, "But we never fought." When handled appropriately, all conflict can end up with very positive results, which moves people closer together.

Here are some of our key do's and don'ts for conflict resolution. I use these same points both in my personal and business life to help build relationships.

1) *We do not avoid conflict.* When there is an issue we will discuss it right away, even if we really would rather not. This does not suggest we search for reasons to disagree, but we are in tune with the other person enough to feel when something is genuinely wrong.

2) *Questions.* We ask lots of skillful, non-accusatory, non-confrontational questions. The goal is to dig down to the REAL issue without causing the other person any more pain than necessary, in order to decide upon something we can do to fix it. Asking questions keeps both people talking and thinking, so nobody is able to shut down.

3) *Stay on track.* In the process we occasionally get off track, so we will often remind ourselves of WHY we are arguing. This avoids either person's effort to confuse the issue, which makes resolution difficult. We work as a team to stay focused on the real issue so we can find a productive solution.

4) *Avoid absolutes.* We do our best to avoid using words like Never, Always, and Can't. These are "absolutes" which are seldom true. Nobody ALWAYS does anything. To say you do will make them defensive, shut down, or feel the need to lash back at the other person by bringing up how you NEVER do _____. The discussion becomes a tennis match going back and forth, while accomplishing nothing productive.

We strive not to get overly dramatic in an effort to win.

5) *No prior bad acts.* We have learned it is very destructive to bring up prior times one of us did something unrelated to the issue at hand to make the other person seem weaker. It is NOT about winning. When I bring something up from the past to "get one up" on Debbie, it will only make her feel bad and shut down. How is this helping our relationship grow?

6) *Empathy.* We genuinely make an effort to see the issue from the other person's point of view. This can be very hard when the passion rises. This is when I most need to employ emotional neutrality, lowering my voice and altering my body language so I come across as someone who cares about her position. I genuinely want to understand what she is saying. Only then can I learn so together we can find a productive resolution. I begin a lot of statements with, "I understand where you are coming from ..." Often I also say, "So if I hear what you are saying correctly, you mean ..." Statements like these keep the other person engaged instead of withdrawn. Plus I just might learn something.

D. <u>Moments and Memories.</u> Many years ago I came to Debbie with an idea. We would no longer buy each other gifts for birthdays, Christmas, Valentine's Day, or any other time when society says we should exchange gifts. Instead this would provide us an opportunity to create memories. I told her there is no way I will remember the watch she gave me for my 25th birthday when I am 65 years old. Because we can buy whatever we want, whenever we want to, what is the point of buying into society's pressure to consume when we are told it is time to say "I love you?" This made sense to her and so we have never bought a *required* gift for each other since. We have instead created so many fun memories to relive as we enjoy the rest of our lives together.

Here is one small example of what I mean; I called it "Operation Anniversary 2000." I wrote a sappy love poem for our sixth wedding anniversary and at 4 a.m. painted one verse onto each of several neon-colored pieces of tag board. I stapled them to pieces of wood for support and then proceeded to nail them to telephone poles stretching the length of the route she drove to her office. She got into her car and there awaited a single red rose with the entire poem typed out on a piece of paper and laminated, so she could follow along while she drove. Every half mile or so, there was another verse on another telephone pole. She loved it. To this day I wonder what all of the thousands of other commuters must have thought that morning. She of course told her girlfriends about it and this made her even happier with me because now she feels even more special every time she gets to tell the story. This gift of a *memory* keeps on giving forever, versus giving a *thing* from which the feeling ends shortly thereafter. This is a simple promise and commitment we made years ago that will pay dividends for the rest of our lives as we laugh into our old age together.

2. **My business and life coach, William Bailey.** Having someone you trust who has been there and done that is invaluable. William Bailey has been building successful businesses for more than 50 years. He has earned the respect of his peers and has been awarded the Horatio Alger Award by Dr. Norman Vincent Peale. Through him I learned what it was like to meet Pope Paul VI, become friends with Ray Kroc, and pal around with Mohammed Ali. My coach has forgotten more about life than I know and that motivates

me to learn from his wisdom. In my lifestyle vehicle, Mr. Bailey rides in the back seat on the passenger's side. From this vantage point he has a clear picture of where the vehicle is headed and can, whenever necessary, advise me on what is most likely coming up ahead on the road, because he has been this way before. And when he is not needed right away, he can relax, drink coffee and watch the DVD player.

A great coach helps you to believe you can be more and is able to teach you HOW to get there. He is a valuable guide on my journey. Before getting Mr. Bailey to coach me I had sought direction from others and they did not help me much. I studied people closely and ended up learning that much of what I was being taught either was untrue or they did not apply it in their own lives. One coach who supposedly had my best interest at heart told me to leave Debbie because she was getting in my way too much.

Without a coach, I grew tired of feeling as though I was wandering in the fog, slowly swerving my vehicle from one shoulder of the road to the other, sometimes temporarily going into the ditch. Without a guide you can trust, making the journey to your ideal lifestyle will be very hard at best and may even become impossible. Mr. Bailey helps me to maximize my time, emotional energy, and experience, to deliberately direct these assets where they will pay off the most, so I can be as productive as possible. If I had not wandered so long in the fog, learning by trial and error, I would be much further on my own personal journey. But there is a saying, "When the student is ready, the master will appear." When I was ready, he appeared, willing and ready to help. Seek out your own Mr. Bailey. Do whatever is necessary to get him/her to take you under their wing and your life will never be the same!

THE $100,000,000 MARCH · *97*

3. **My Entrepreneurs' Organization Forum.** When you are the owner of a business, you should not become too close to your staff. There are four F's of leadership – be firm, fair, and friendly, but do not become familiar. Your spouse will eventually get tired of you talking shop all the time and sadly you will begin to outgrow your friends as you become more and more successful. As you drive down the road, you must choose who you will take with you and who you will leave behind. As an entrepreneur, I had no one to really connect with who understood the challenges unique to being the owner. Few people know what it feels like to be at the top of the corporate pyramid, so I searched for others who did. During my search I found one of the most powerful members of my team, an organization. I heard about this worldwide group of entrepreneurs called EO (Entrepreneurs' Organization).

EO is a group of like-minded successful business owners who seek to enrich each other's lives. The fact that a business-person must EARN membership made it even more attractive to me. You cannot join unless you own the business AND you can prove it is producing at a certain level of revenue. Being a part of a group of other successful entrepreneurs has opened my eyes to so much. I grew up in the 80's, during the Cold War, being told I should hate the Russians. One day in 2003, I was at an EO black-tie affair in Australia talking over drinks with a Russian entrepreneur who was taught to hate Americans as a child. I am blown away by moments like this because I was a small-town boy who started with nothing, and now I travel the world and learn from the best entrepreneurs out there.

EO as a whole is great, but the best part is Forum, a local group of EO members who meet monthly and go on exciting retreats twice a year. I found a group that accepts me for who I am and in which I am able to talk confidentially about both business and personal issues. When you have a strong group of other successful people surrounding you, life does not seem so tough.

Did you ever notice how you tend to play at the same level of your competition? I chose to surround myself with other people who are *more* successful than I am, in order to challenge me to think differently and continue to grow as a person. I need to learn what they are doing that's different so I can implement this knowledge in my life. This group of men has changed my life and I have not missed a single meeting since 2003. This is the level of commitment my Forum demands, as do all of my key team members, together we help each other live fulfilling lives.

5.6   People Studies

What does this mean? Why should I do it?

People Studies is the process of understanding why people do what they do and the art of applying this understanding to affect other people's behavior, so all parties achieve a win-win result.

Why study people?

I believe that every single thing I could want to

> **DO**   (skydive, become a millionaire, drive a racecar, fly into space, find the perfect spouse, be a great parent, etc.) or

> **HAVE** (money, fame, business ownership, well-behaved children, supportive friends, fancy house, own my own Caribbean island, etc.),

somebody has already done it or has it! This belief inspires me to learn from those around me at all times. When you have what I want, it means you know something I don't. So I will create a win-win situation to motivate you to teach me what you know. Then I will absorb the information like a sponge, assimilate it into my own lifestyle plan, and then apply the knowledge, mimicking the patterns of other successful people. A witty guy in one of the business training sessions I used to lead suggested that everybody in the room should just become a *Clone-A-Bush*.

You do not have to reinvent the wheel in order to succeed. Just copy what I am teaching you, and you should certainly do at least as well if not better than I have. The student should always surpass the teacher, so long as the teacher teaches both what they did right AND what they did wrong. When the student adds their own natural God-given talents to what they have been taught, they should do better than the teacher. Intelligence is good but wisdom is better. Intelligence is learning from your own personal experiences, which is OK but painfully slow. However, wisdom is learning from someone else's experiences, so you not only benefit from their successful choices but are able to avoid their mistakes.

In order to build your lifestyle teams, you must be able to effectively work with many varieties of people over a long period of time. I will never *graduate* because I have committed to make my entire life a never-ending course in People Studies. The more people I study, the more I am completely certain both success and failure result from one's own mental patterns. How a person FEELS about something determines whether they will act or not, and not taking action is still action. The actions we take, or fail to take, will determine our habits in life. Our habits are our personal patterns of success or failure and over time, they develop into what makes us who we are. How we think and what we do are immensely influenced by the people we choose or allow to surround us. Choose poorly to your own life's detriment. I cannot stress this enough. People Studies is a skill everyone can develop and one you must have in order to make the journey to your ideal lifestyle.

5.7 People Principles

In order to enjoy my ideal lifestyle, I must help others get what they want and be as productive at this as possible at all times. I have a great deal of urgency because I have much to accomplish in my life and the clock is ticking. In order to optimize my efforts, I follow these principles of People Studies in every deal I do.

1. Self-Study. The first and most important person to study is you. Over time I have learned my natural talents and weaknesses. I then began surrounding myself with people who were gifted in ways I was not, instead of attempting to become a jack-of-all-trades. I was honest about what I liked and what I didn't. I did not allow myself to feel bad just because something was not my strength. By being honest and then seeking out others who were better than me in certain areas, I allowed myself to specialize in what I enjoyed and was very good at. I ended up with more time and money than ever before. I acted deliberately in order to maximize my income and personal satisfaction.

   I have found that most people make most of their decisions based on emotion instead of logic and that a decision motivated by a negative emotion (fear, jealousy, anger, etc.) is usually a wrong decision. One of the most critical elements to becoming successful for me was to learn to control my own emotions in order to make better decisions from an emotionally-neutral mindset. This has both made me prosperous and happily fulfilled.

2. <u>Quick Judgments.</u> I learned to make **correct** quick judgments of what other people would most likely do or think based upon the understanding they are just trying to get what they need and are most likely highly emotional. I now make these judgments based upon experience derived from intense study of People Patterns – consistent, cyclical, repetitious behaviors. I made many mistakes over the years but because my financial vehicle was strong and commitment to succeed powerful, I always was able to bounce back. There is truth to the adage that says whatever doesn't kill you will make you stronger. Then again this is true only when you learn from your mistakes.

The study of patterns is just another guide to use to make better decisions. I stress to you to use whatever People Studies tools you can in order to make the best decisions possible for your life, no matter what anyone else says. The more good choices you make, the better your lifestyle will be. Even though understanding group patterns helps, I seek to find the truth about the individual. Each person deserves to be judged upon their own merits. Be bold enough to be honest and willing to see the truth in each person. Fortune always favors the bold!

3. <u>Create Win-Win Situations.</u> People are relatively easy to understand. Everybody, without exception, wants a better life. What *better* means is, of course, different for everyone but the truth remains, they want *better*. I just need to figure out what their definition of better is – what do they want? Then I do my best to create a win-win situation so both of us get what we desire. My focus is to help them get whatever <u>emotional</u> or <u>physical</u> stuff they want. I create opportunities for them to win and as a result of their winning, so do I. I am not selfless, don't misunderstand. I am deliberate and strategic, but my genuine desire is to create a positive outcome for both parties.

4. <u>Reputation.</u> Your word is your bond. My grandfather said a man's word is all he leaves behind when he dies – either he kept it or he didn't. It is nearly impossible to create win-win situations without a good reputation because even when you have a good deal for someone, they will most likely not trust you enough to even listen. I have never bounced a check. I always pay people what they are owed and do what I say I will – period! Therefore, people trust me and are willing to take on risk with me. I believe it is because they know what they are getting in the deal! I strive for few surprises. Some always seem to occur, but the more experience you get, the fewer surprises pop up. And when a surprise occurs, NEVER run. Deal with it quickly and to the best of your ability, even if it means you take a personal or business loss. More money can always be made but a person's reputation is very tough to rebuild! I have long judged others more by what they did when something went wrong and how they dealt with the challenge than by what they did when all went well.

Here is an example of this point. By late 1998 I felt invincible because I was young and completely debt-free. Life was very good, but then I thought that just because I was successful in one business arena, I would automatically be great in another. To make a long and painful story short, I started with nothing, made a lot of money, and then lost all of it plus hundreds of thousands more. By mid-1999 life seemed very dark and desperate. I was faced with a choice, which turned out to be one of the most significant of my life. Should I take the easy way out and declare bankruptcy, or should I start all over again and rebuild?

I really only thought of what my grandfather had told me, and the decision was obvious, but still not easy to swallow. I laid off staff, cut expenses to the bare bone, and started over. How I look back on this moment now is that life was challenging me to see what I was really made of. I really was not starting from square one because I had built it all once before, so deep down I felt I could do it again. But my ego and confidence took a huge hit. Luckily I was surrounded by a handful of people who believed in me more than I did myself at that time. It took me 39 months (3 ¼ years) but I paid everybody back in full what they were owed and was once again debt-free. I could have walked away from many of the debts because they were business-related. But my logic was that they extended credit to me, and I agreed to accept the product and/or service. Therefore I owed them the money.

Every single one of those business people, vendors, and staff that I dealt with during this process is STILL with me almost 10 years later. Surprises happen, but how you deal with them is really what makes you who you are. Every day for the rest of my life, I get to look in the mirror and know I did the right thing, no matter how I felt about it at the time. I chose to take the Path of Performance and keep my integrity, instead of the much easier Path of Excuses. I did not seek the government's help or retain a slick bankruptcy attorney to try to get me out of the challenge I had gotten myself into. I made the right decision, and climbed the money mountain another time. My final point here is that having money is a heck of a lot better than not – you ought to try it out!!!

5. Empathy versus Sympathy. I started my travels like most, showing SYMPATHY for others. I really did not know any better. I have seen countless people feel sorry for themselves and others who have failed at the game of life because of their own foolish mistakes. I now believe being sympathetic is pathetic. When you offer a shoulder to cry on, who does this help? It helps the person with the shoulder, who feels empowered and significant because they are important enough for this other person to come to with their problems. But they seldom if ever actually help the crier to better their situation.

Instead, I now choose to show EMPATHY. I believe empathy is the process of understanding the other person's situation, listening openly and remaining as emotionally neutral as possible without getting sucked in, and offering realistic experience-based solutions to solve the challenge. Instead of dishing out opinions, the empathetic person shares their relevant life experience or points the other to someone else who can offer actual life experience to overcome the challenge. Empathy is about helping people lift themselves up, instead of just allowing them to continue to whine and stay stationary. Sympathy is used often as a tool to control, while empathy helps the individual become more self-sufficient, thereby assisting them to be more independent.

In order to effectively build win-win situations, I have to be an empathetic leader instead of a sympathetic follower. I believe that by making this choice, I can create a positive *ripple* effect, like a stone thrown into a pond, by helping others elevate themselves rather than becoming a part of their problems. I support each of my team members in any way I can, so long as the individual does NOT detract from my journey.

6. Put your cards on the table. Be clear from the beginning. Be upfront. Never purposefully mislead others and constantly remain aware of the details in the human process – you are building a flashcard mental library from which you will draw upon for the rest of your life. If you make a mistake, accept accountability and apologize, then make it right and move on. This is a major reason why sales skills have helped me so much because sales is just effective communication.

7. High Expectations. I am tough on myself, tougher than I tend to be on other people. Therefore since I am going to hold myself accountable to a certain standard of doing things, I must be strict with those around me as well. When

someone tells me they will do ___ by ___ for $ ___, they had better fulfill what they have agreed to, or else. If *surprises* occur, I expect constant communication to keep me informed. Why?

There are two reasons. First, it is human nature to start thinking the worst when things go wrong. An abundance of open, honest, and emotionally-neutral communication becomes critical to continue productively moving forward. Second, I am accountable to all those other people who are parts of the deal, to whom I made certain promises. I will not allow other people's poor planning or lax character to negatively affect mine! That is unacceptable. I have consumed far too many aspirin to get to where I am to expect any less from those around me.

Open, honest communication at the start of the process to establish clear expectations of the deal is crucial to a successful conclusion of the deal. Continued communication during the process helps to hold everyone accountable to what was agreed, overcome challenges, and build the relationships necessary for future deals.

8. <u>Quantity.</u> Do as many deals as you are able to successfully complete. The more deals you do, the more human experience you will gain. Every single deal is different and is an opportunity to learn, experience, and grow more. Each deal helps you to gain mental momentum which will prepare you emotionally to tackle the bigger deals coming in the future.

9. <u>Proactive.</u> Sales is the art of showing empathy while asking skillful questions and making skillful statements in order to get an agreement from the customer, then remain persistent enough to close the deal. Sales has taught me to become very good at anticipating both good and bad. Whenever possible I will overcome potential objections or challenges before

they ever come up. The more experience I gain, the easier this becomes. Assume the worst and then do something to prevent it.

10. <u>Be honest.</u> Don't fool yourself. Be willing to call it as you see it. A crook is a crook and I will separate myself quickly and completely the moment I have proof that someone is destructive either to the deal or my lifestyle journey. I have to because I cannot afford to have their poor choices negatively reflect upon me. Think about it. If you enrolled a duck in eagle school, dressed him like an eagle, taught him to screech like an eagle, got him to walk like and talk like an eagle, what would you really have at the end of the day? Just a duck pretending to be an eagle.

I have worked hard to develop the skill to be able to spot the eagle that life has cruelly disguised as a duck. Fear, negative thinking and the lack of a good EST leads to eagles going through life allowing themselves to remain disguised as ducks. I love helping them learn what they really are deep inside because once they do, their natural eagle instincts will take over. Given the right coaching and enough time, they will emerge as eagles and begin to soar!

11. <u>Ask. Listen. Think.</u> In order to effectively study people you must be willing to:

A. <u>Ask a lot of pointed, deliberate questions.</u> I started out very shy when I was 18 but by necessity I gradually got over it. I had no other option. People won't typically just come to me and tell me their life's story unless there is something wrong with them. But I need to know details in order to make good decisions about the people I am dealing with, so I must ask deliberate, possibly embarrassing questions.

B. <u>Genuinely listen to the answers they give.</u> I strive to feel whatever it is they are feeling. Do not get this confused with being sympathetic. My objective is to better understand the other person, so I may better create the win-win. Share the experience with them but keep your wits. It is difficult to help when you are feeling their pain as your own because you will have a very tough time remaining emotionally neutral. I just make sure I am totally engaged with them, tune out all distractions, including even taking off my watch, and focus upon discovering what the other person really needs.

C. <u>Constantly ask yourself how you can help.</u> During all of my communication with the other person, I am thinking out scenarios in which I can leverage my existing team, personal experience, or other resources to assist them. When I am confident I can help, then I will create a deal in which both of us win.

5.8 Personal Character

Again, the first person to study is you. Successful people can often read others like a book, and to them little matters more than someone's character. They see through the frauds quickly and separate from them just as fast. In order to get successful people willing to teach you, you must be someone they want to associate with. Therefore, developing your character is critical to aligning yourself with others who can help you succeed.

I found on my journey that developing a personal Code of Honor was very useful. This helped me keep my internal compass always pointing in the right direction and to resist temptations that would have otherwise gotten me off track on my lifestyle quest. It helped me keep my vehicle between the lines on the road. None of us is perfect all the time, but having a code can help get you through some tough times. I created an acronym of *FAIL CHAP IF* from the first letters of each key point in my code because I believe if I stray from this code I will eventually fail.

Here is my personal Code of Honor.

1. **Freedom.** I must live free to choose in order to enjoy my ideal lifestyle.

2. **Accountability.** I will not blame others for my losses, nor allow credit for my wins to be stolen because my life is my own responsibility.

3. **Integrity.** I will strive to do what is right, regardless of how I feel about it.

4. **Leadership.** I will be an example to follow, not a warning sign. I believe leadership is about elevating others, not a popularity contest.

5. **Commitment.** I will constantly seek opportunities to improve myself and those closest to me both physically and mentally.

6. **Honesty.** I will do right by all I deal with. Character overshadows all else.

7. **Accessibility.** I will do my best to be accessible to those I serve.

8. **Performance.** Life only pays me for what I do, not what I say or hope I will do.

9. **Inspirational.** I will inspire others by focusing upon what I CAN do and taking action, rather than making excuses to justify my failures.

10. **Fulfillment.** I will do what I say, when I say I will do it – period.

You have come a long way already since we began. I suspect you understand where you are starting from much better now and who you will allow to travel along with you. Once you are excited and ready to begin traveling, you will need a comprehensive success process in order to achieve whatever you desire. Your fulfillment formula must be simple to understand and, when implemented properly, must consistently produce winning results. All great journeys start with the first step...

5.9 Truth # 5 Action Points

Making your lifestyle journey a successful one depends upon your people skills. Everything you want is closely tied to communicating and relating effectively with others and developing strong, lasting relationships with good people. All of your dreams are possible, with the help of the right people. How do you get the right people in the right places, to join your lifestyle quest?

A. <u>Get yourself in the right environment.</u> Give yourself the greatest chance for success by choosing the right location to start your journey. Great military leaders have always known that whoever chooses the battlefield holds an immediate and significant advantage. Be willing to temporarily go it alone, if necessary, as you search for answers to determine *who you really are*. Eliminate all distractions that currently drag you down or hold you back.

B. <u>Build your teams.</u> Success is a team sport and none of us makes it alone. Begin to set up your Emotional Support, Peak Performance, and Task-Doer teams right away from the good people currently surrounding you. In order to most productively invest your time, emotional energy, and experience you need numerous team members. Just as each tool in a toolbox has a unique purpose, so does each team member. As you move along the Path of Performance, constantly add new and better supporters, advisors, and workers. Emotional neutrality is key in order to effectively build and lead productive teams. Judge only by results – hire slowly and fire fast!

C. <u>Make your life a career in People Studies.</u> Sales is effective communication of one's beliefs and business is effective people-relations. Everything we do involves people.

Everything you want is within your grasp with the right people assisting you. To get people willing to help you win, you must help them win. Reputation and personal character are paramount to getting others to trust in you. As a result of studying people, other successful people will be willing to teach you what they did to succeed so you can copy them. Enjoying your ideal lifestyle requires helping many others live better as well.

TRUTH # 6

The higher your Life GPA, the more enjoyable your lifestyle.

Your life's GPA is your *Success Score*. Your GPA is your ability to consistently achieve whatever you set your mind to. Just as in school, the more successful students usually have a higher GPA. As someone's GPA increases, typically so do the opportunities made available to them in life.

However, your **Life** GPA is more important than any ever earned in school because now your Life GPA will determine your lifestyle. Where you live, how much money you are worth, how much free time you have and how you will spend it, the car you drive, how safe and secure is the environment you create for your family, your relationship with your spouse and children, your health, and so much more are ALL results of your Life GPA. A high Life GPA = a high quality of life!

When you learn how to implement the following *Life Fulfillment Formula* properly, your ideal lifestyle becomes merely a matter of time and effort. Success is the repeatable systematic process of finding a way to WIN, no matter what surprises life may have in store for you. Study and copy the achievement patterns of the successful and you too can earn whatever they earn. Here is my own personal recipe for achievement.

1. Make a firm <u>Decision.</u>
2. Develop a successful person's <u>Mindset.</u>
3. Rid yourself of <u>Distractions.</u>
4. Find and secure the right team members, especially a personal <u>Coach.</u>
5. <u>Visualize</u> and thereby expect victory.
6. Understand and use the power of <u>Mental Momentum.</u>
7. Set a <u>Goal.</u>
8. Develop a <u>Plan.</u>
9. Take immediate <u>Action</u> to consistently overpower inertia.
10. Efficiently <u>Track</u> progress.
11. Quickly <u>Evaluate</u> performance.
12. Instantly <u>Change</u> your plan when necessary.
13. Appropriately <u>Reward</u> results.
14. Accurately <u>Record</u> important process details.
15. Overcome <u>Fear.</u>
16. And remain <u>Disciplined</u> and <u>Persistent</u> until YOUR goal is achieved.

I have already written at great length about decisions, mindset, distractions, team building, and coach acquisition. This truth will cover visualization, mental momentum, goal setting, planning, taking action, tracking, evaluation, change, rewards, and recording. I will focus upon fear, discipline, and persistence within the Truths yet to come.

6.1   Visualization

First conceived, then achieved. Going back as far as I can remember, something I have always done is visualize myself accomplishing my goal. No matter what I was seeking to achieve, when I sat alone and visualized victory, I *felt* it. I felt what it was going to be like when I won. I saw the end of the race in my mind's eye. I played it over and over like a movie from start to finish.

This is a skill I have developed to the point where I can virtually see and intensely feel the win as if it has already occurred. As a result, victory becomes a foregone conclusion, simply a matter of implementing my formula once again. Once my decision is made, achieving my desire starts with the mental image of winning, because if I do not feel excited and ready to get started after visualizing my victory, then I have to ask myself if this is really important to me. I believe I should have butterflies in my stomach and a burning desire to win in order to be able to create enough emotional energy to overcome the obstacles life is sure to throw at me.

Take the time to visualize your victory every single day leading up to and during your goal pursuit. It is easy and effective. Visualization is the process of conditioning your mind to picture success and thereby expect to win. You gradually develop the ability to instantly control how you feel, tune out any and all negative distractions, and remain focused on what needs to be done in order to win. Historically, great warriors, athletes, and business people have used this technique to consistently triumph.

This is what I do:

1. Right environment. I find a quiet spot so I can close my eyes and visualize without distraction.

2. Mental imagery. I ask myself over and over what it will feel and look like when I "cross the finish line and experience my victory." Who will be with me, what will I be wearing, how will the weather look, etc.? I am striving for as much detail as possible. Then I write these images down and review them if I get discouraged to help refresh my focus and excitement.

3. Visual aids. I will collect visual aids I can look at regularly to help me keep the vision fresh. For example, when I had wanted a specific car, I went to the dealership and picked up brochures. Then I cut out the pictures of what I planned to achieve and put them in places where I could regularly see them (i.e. on my bathroom mirror, rearview mirror, and in my office). I even laminated a copy and carried it with me at all times. My objective was to keep the prize in front of me as often as possible to keep me focused and believing I would earn it.

4. Break negative patterns. If any self-doubt or other mental garbage pops in my head while visualizing my victory, I will open my eyes, stand up, and shake my arms out. This removes the weeds from your field by breaking your negative mental patterns. This is much like scratching a mental CD. When you do it enough times, the CD won't play any longer. Over time, by repeatedly pulling out the mental weeds, they will eventually die, which allows you to replace them with good seeds. Once I have interrupted my negative mental pattern, I will sit back down and start the visualization process over. Maintaining the negative thought pattern and allowing the mental weeds to remain

will likely choke off any good seeds as they begin to grow. A key element in developing your rich-person's mindset is controlling and directing what you are willing to think about and eliminating everything else. Focus your energy properly – like a laser beam.

5. <u>Feel the win.</u> Over time, the vision becomes crystal clear. I know everything that will occur and most importantly HOW IT WILL MAKE ME FEEL. We are driven by our feelings, so I do my best to allow myself to FEEL THE WIN before it has even occurred. This creates the expectation of the win and when I expect to, I win.

6. <u>Repetition.</u> Then I play this mental movie every morning and when needed during the day. It quickly becomes a habit. Every time I do this, I feel more energized and ready to take on the world. This process makes me feel like a winner and when you feel like a winner you are more likely to perform like one, so get yourself in the right mental place to win and stay there.

By developing the ability to put yourself in the right mindset for victory, you have learned to control your greatest asset. Your mind is your most powerful tool to enjoying your ideal lifestyle. Negative people and other challenges will pop up from time to time. By staying the course and keeping focused on the prize, you will win much more than you lose. Eventually almost nothing will bother you and winning will become the only acceptable habit for you.

6.2   Mental Momentum/Confidence

Visualization of victory puts us on the starting block of making our goal a reality. Mental Momentum is what gets us going when the gun fires, and keeps us going until we win. Mental

Momentum is the feeling of knowing you will win, by virtue of the fact that you have entered the race. This is an awesome feeling and built over time, one win after another. We cannot change the laws of nature, such as momentum and inertia. Natural laws are just too powerful. However, we CAN understand and use them to achieve what we desire.

Momentum	*Is the property of a <u>moving body</u> which determines the length of time required to bring it to rest when under the action of an opposing constant force and <u>has the power to speed up or slow down at an ever-increasing pace</u>.*

Can we really become unstoppable?

I believe the answer is YES, and this is why. When I finally understood momentum and how much power it has to affect our lives either positively or negatively, my life changed forever. I cannot overstate the significance of this realization. Momentum increases exponentially as a body moves, which makes it harder and harder for opposing forces to stop or even slow the body. I hypothesized that my mental momentum is the same as my confidence. And therefore as my confidence grew so would my success at an ever-increasing pace, because eventually nothing would be able to stop me. I set out to prove my hypothesis, in order to fully *sell* myself to believe it. This is how I did it. To convince myself that my confidence could grow to the point of me being unstoppable, I had to first prove my feelings had mass. Why?

FEELINGS determine actions. Actions determine results. Results determine my confidence level. Therefore how I feel will eventually determine my level of Mental Momentum and

Confidence. The laws of nature state that only a moving body can develop momentum. For something to be considered a moving body, it must have mass. I learned that a study had been done to prove that *feelings have energy*. Stanford University did a study in which people were hooked up to machines to measure the energy given off by their brains. The study showed that when we experience intense feelings there is measurable energy given off. This made a lot of sense to me. What do you feel when someone who is angry comes into a room? When you are around someone who is out-of-this-world excited, do you get excited as well? We cannot help it because other people's emotions are contagious. This is why we must be careful about who we allow to surround us. Our mental field gets massive amounts of input consciously and subconsciously all the time. Our mind is like a sponge soaking up everything around us. OK, so feelings have energy, but do they have mass?

Einstein said Energy equals Mass times the Speed of Light squared ($E = mc2$), which proves that if something has energy it also has mass. By proving feelings have energy, they also have mass, and something that has mass can develop momentum and can only be slowed down by an opposing force. Therefore I concluded, my confidence CAN become unstoppable and the only opposing force that can slow me down is <u>mental friction</u>.

How do you overcome mental friction and grow your momentum?

Every time you overcome an obstacle, achieve a goal, prove a negative person wrong, etc., you gain confidence, which is emotional Mental Momentum. As we begin to move faster and faster in one direction, we pick up speed by facing and beating all of the opposing forces again and again. So long as we have picked the *correct* direction and continue to push on no matter what, our success is assured. People's lives can spiral in either direction – good or bad. By making the decision which direction your life will head in, you have set your vehicle on the right path to eventual ideal lifestyle enjoyment. Nature requires that mental **friction** (fear, negative people, limiting beliefs) must always exist and constantly attempt to slow us down, but as you gain **confidence** your mind becomes more and more unstoppable, until finally almost nothing life throws at you has a chance to be anything more than just another bump in the road. How do you build your Mental Momentum muscle? How do you become so confident that life can no longer stop you and struggles to even briefly slow you down? By improving your life GPA, that's how!

6.3   Goal Setting

I have read many books that discussed this topic and they all taught basically the same message. Without a goal, you do not have a point to focus on hitting, much like blindfolding someone, then handing them a dart and telling them to throw it hoping to hit the bulls' eye. The likelihood of even coming close to the dartboard is poor, but to hit the dead center of the board without proper aiming is next to impossible. I agree that we need to set goals, but more importantly, we need to *achieve* goals.

6.3.1 What is a GOAL?

A goal IS a clearly defined objective. A goal is NOT anticipated to happen, hoped for, or wished to be. A goal IS expected to occur because when approached properly, accomplishment is only a matter of time and effort. A goal IS like a single stair within a tall staircase and a life dream is represented by the landing at the top. Therefore, you must achieve numerous goals in order to obtain a dream.

I will illustrate this point by using a dream of mine as an 11-year old. I decided I needed to become an Eagle Scout in the Boy Scouts of America. When I first was given my Boy Scout Handbook and looked at all of the ranks, skill awards, and merit badges I was required to earn on my path to Eagle Scout, it appeared a daunting task. Each rank was made up of smaller Action Steps (bite-size pieces), as was each skill award and merit badge. Therefore, every single rank, skill award or merit badge I earned was like taking one single step up the staircase toward Eagle, which was at the top just waiting for me. Even though the dream seemed overwhelming, I took the process one bite at a time. Before I knew it, I had earned my Tenderfoot, 2nd Class, 1st Class and on and on I climbed one stair at a time. To this day, I give Boy Scouts a great deal of credit for my life success because of what I learned on my journey to Eagle. I learned how to sell, communicate, lead, manage, and so much more. I was part of a team, which helped me to build my character and strengthen my mental muscle. Because of the BSA's coaching, process of setting goals, developing plans, and taking actions, I did earn my Eagle Scout at age 15. The men and women who invest their time and energy into shaping the lives of young men deserve significant amounts of praise for what they do. I am living proof of what can happen with the right direction and coaching.

6.3.2 Prepare to WIN – How to properly create your GOAL

Achieving goals is not a mystery nor is it really that hard. Achieving a goal is much like sitting down for dinner to eat an entire elephant, which can be overwhelming until you get your mind around the task by breaking the elephant into bite-size pieces. I so often see people make the mistake of biting off more than they can chew, quickly becoming overwhelmed, and quitting.

Start out to win. Set your goals correctly from the beginning and you will find accomplishing them a methodical, systematic process which you will be able to duplicate over and over no matter what goal you want to achieve. Accomplishing what you want will be as easy as shooting fish in a barrel.

6.3.3 A properly set goal must be

1. <u>Challenging yet Attainable.</u> You must be inspired to push yourself outside your normal comfort zone in order to grow, but not so much you get overwhelmed and quit. You must stretch yourself and be challenged in order to keep your interest, or you will quickly get bored and possibly quit. Imagine going to the gym and continually curling a five-pound dumbbell. You would get bored because of lack of results, then lose interest quickly and quit. The same example can be used if you pick up an 80-pound dumbbell and attempt to curl that – too much! The objective is to gradually stretch your mind, but not so far or so fast that you break. Take it right to your current limit's edge and then slightly further to gradually expand your limits. A great coach will help you with this process. The amazing thing is, once you stretch your mind it will NEVER go back to its original position. Your mind will be expanded forever. Just like building a physical muscle, this is a gradual process of personal growth, pushing yourself past prior self-imposed limits and ultimately achieving your ideal lifestyle.

2. <u>Well-Researched.</u> You must be aware of all of the dynamics that could affect your goal's achievement. A great coach is invaluable with this because they have been there and done it before. A good personal trainer knows what you will need to do, how your body will react, and all of the other forces at work in getting into

shape. A business coach will help you understand all of the critical elements to insuring successful completion of your objective. But I have found that for my own sanity, blind faith no longer works for me. For example, if my goal is to lose weight, then I need to understand what my BMR (Basal Metabolic Rate) is and how it affects me, plus any other important details. Researching your objective and the best path to getting there is key to your level of dedication to achieving it. Again, knowledge is like light to a dark room. Education inspires belief that you can do it. The more you believe you will reach your goal, the greater the likelihood of getting there.

Another very important element of researching your goal is to understand who or what will be the most likely obstacles you will need to overcome. Does your goal involve beating others in a competition? If so, you must know your competitor as well as possible. Does your goal involve earning a certain amount of money or buying something specific? There will be obstacles or challenges on the path to achieving any goal. The better you anticipate the challenges and prepare for them in advance, the greater likelihood of your achieving the goal by your deadline.

3. Specifically Defined (Measurable / Numeric / Quantifiable). You need to know exactly what you are going to achieve. Your goal cannot be a vague concept, such as being happy or rich, or you set yourself up from the start for disappointment. One person's definition of being happy or rich is totally different from another's. Your goal must be a specific item you want to purchase, ($200,000 house), amount of money you want to earn ($10,000), or a number of pounds you want to lose (20 pounds), etc. Your goal must be able to be described in numeric terms. When your goal is a NUMBER, you can direct all of

your efforts at one exact target, then set up daily bite-size Action Points to get there, and finally be able to track your progress easily so you can adjust if necessary. Set yourself up to win by clearly defining with a numeric value what success IS! Now success is a matter of planning and action, not a vague shot in the dark.

4. <u>Written down.</u> By the simple but powerful act of writing your goal down on paper, you have consciously AND subconsciously decided upon and physically committed to its achievement. You have given concrete form to an intangible desire. Whatever you commit to can be achieved. This should be done using a single sentence or phrase stating with absolute clarity and certainty what you will accomplish. Write this on the top of your Goal Performance Chart (GPC), which I will explain in detail later. When you put it to paper, your mind will find ways to take action and get it done, instead of making excuses to justify staying stationary. To help you stay focused and on track, carry your GPC and Planning Calendar (PC) with you everywhere.

5. <u>Verbally committed to.</u> Tell all of the supportive people around you, who will hold you accountable, what you will achieve and by when. Your coach, spouse, and friends are all great sources of accountability. When you commit and succeed, your credibility will increase and your all-important reputation will improve. You never know who you might need to participate with you on your next Success Team. By building your reputation as a *doer*, more people will want to take part in your future endeavors, which will make them easier to accomplish. When you have committed to those around you and do NOT reach the goal, these same people will ask you "why?" and maybe tease you forever, or worst of all just think of you as another *talker*. By committing your intentions to the

world, you have left yourself no option but to accomplish the goal. Winning has now become a must, because your honor is on the line!

6. Supported with Reasons. You must know WHY achieving this goal is important to you. How will reaching this goal make you feel? Write your reasons down along with the goal itself to be accomplished. Give as many emotionally charged reasons as possible why you are going to get this done. The more emotional the reasons, the more powerful your drive will be to achieve the goal. Your emotional energy is the juice in your vehicle's battery – it is what gets you started and energizes you on your journey.

7. Punctuated with an absolute Deadline. Along with your reasons, you need a rigid deadline. When you say to yourself and mean it, "I must do ___ by ___ date", you will find a way to win because failure is NOT an option. Your deadline must be reasonable. You did not get fat or broke overnight, so it is unfair to expect yourself to lose the weight or get rich overnight. Give yourself enough time to grow. Set yourself up to win with proper expectations. Reasons and deadlines create an internal sense of urgency, a burning desire, which will cause incredible amounts of emotional energy to be generated so you can direct it toward attaining your goal.

8. Charted. You need a visual tool to track your progress. This is more than just writing down the objective, "I will lose 20 pounds." You will take it a step further by breaking it down to specific daily Action and Progress Steps (bite size pieces), put them on a chart you can color in, and visually evaluate your performance daily. Use your own variation of the examples I have included for you. A visual reference makes it easy to see your strengths and weaknesses in order to adjust your plan when necessary.

6.4   Planning

A goal without a plan is a mere wish and wishes won't pay the rent. You can talk about what you will do until you are blue in the face, but you will struggle to achieve any goal without a proper plan. Developing the plan is laying out the daily *performance* (Action and Progress Steps) necessary, weekly Reward and Evaluation Points, and overall sequence of events that have to occur for you to achieve your goal by the deadline.

6.4.1   What is a plan?

A plan is a system of clearly defined steps necessary to achieve your goal laid out in a linear form. A plan is your road map; it shows you your final destination and charts the best way to get there. A plan is the bridge to reaching your goal, because creating a plan requires mapping out how to get from where you are now to where you need to be. A plan is your challenging yet attainable goal broken down into daily Action and Progress Steps defined numerically. A plan is always written down using a Goal Performance Chart, developed with your coach, and punctuated with an unyielding deadline. A plan is completed with weekly Reward and Evaluation Points to ensure you stay on course, by providing small incentives to earn along the journey and make necessary plan adjustments without changing either the goal or deadline. Having a well-prepared road map makes reaching your final destination an inevitable conclusion thereby giving you, the driver, overwhelming confidence on your journey.

6.4.2 Plan = Success Routine

Creating a plan is creating your overall *success routine*. A successful routine answers the question, "What must be done daily, weekly, and monthly to reach this goal by the deadline?" A successful routine maximizes your results by most efficiently directing your time and effort thereby increasing your emotional energy and confidence exponentially. Your routine consists of taking action, measuring progress, and regularly rewarding performance, which will keep you striving for more and more. Repeat the process until your goal is reached. A routine is a pattern, just like a habit, and a person can have either a winning or losing routine. The moment you stop a winning routine, the positive results will begin to dissipate, so when you find a routine that works, stick with it.

However, if your routine drains your energy, slows your momentum, and results in a lack of adequate performance, then the routine (the plan) must be changed in order to get back on track. ALL positions are temporary, whether they are up or down, so never allow yourself to get overly discouraged. Stay focused on the prize, keep your tunnel vision, don't allow distractions to take you off course, and use your PPT to help make necessary plan adjustments. The bottom line is that a successful routine gets results and results are all that matter.

Your Success Routine must possess:

1. Daily bite-size Action and Progress Steps, which when totaled over the time allowed for the goal, will put you slightly over what is required. These steps are recorded and tracked on your GPC.

2. Weekly Reward Points to strive for, which motivate you to accomplish what must be done each week in order to be on track. Small regular rewards are absolutely necessary to remain motivated.

3. Weekly Evaluation Points for study. If progress is on track or off, these pause points allow you the opportunity to see the truth, whatever it may be, and then act accordingly.

6.4.3 Tools to acquire & prepare in advance of GPC completion

1. All necessary **goal preparation** completed to insure your goal has been created properly and will be easy to plan for and take immediate action on.

    Before you set out to make a detailed plan:
    *   Know what you will accomplish.
    *   Do your research to ensure your daily Action and Progress Steps are both challenging and attainable.
    *   Work with your coach to anticipate the most likely challenges so you can prepare in advance.
    *   List the reasons why this goal is important to you.
    *   Decide upon appropriate weekly Rewards Points.
    *   Agree to an unshakeable deadline.

2. **Calendar.** I use the notebook-sized one because I can easily carry it with me in order to jot things down, use as a quick daily reference guide, and plan objectives out months ahead of time.

3. **GPC.** I typically make many mistakes during the GPC creation process, so either I have a lot of blank copies of my GPC or I just do it on the computer. As explained in the following example, this tool will give you the ability to accurately record and track your performance. The number of columns on your GPC will be determined by the number of action- and progress-related tracking items you will need to do in order to achieve your goal. Create one column for EACH individual Action and Progress Step. Notice that in the following example (Section 6.4.42 Bottom half of GPC), only three columns were needed but, in the real-life "Body Fat Loss Competition" example (Section 6.11.3 Final Month), I had to use five (three were action-related and two were progress-related).

4. **Black and Red markers.** I use these colors for specific reasons. Red inspires feelings of urgency, so I use red to show the passing of time. Black represents performance.

6.4.4 How to create your GPC with daily Action and Progress Steps

Your GPC is the tool that automatically provides the structured pattern for the daily action and progress that will lead to successfully accomplishing your goal. When I set out to accomplish any kind of personal or business goal, I use a GPC religiously. It has proved to be an invaluable tool to help me make a lot of money, recover fully from multiple serious injuries, win a body fat loss competition, and achieve numerous other goals. The process of creating your own GPC, for any goal you seek to achieve, is very simple.

I will show you how to create a GPC for any goal by using a simple example to illustrate the basics. Then I will take the GPC and walk you through how to use it to record your performance, track and evaluate your progress, remain flexible enough to change directions when necessary, and ultimately achieve your goal.

Let us say you just started in sales selling small residential appliances by going into the home and working directly with the homeowner. <u>You have learned from your sales manager on average that when someone calls upon a prospective customer, they are able to schedule a demonstration half of the time, and close a sale 60 percent of the time for an average sale of $500.</u> During your Monday morning meeting, your sales manager has given an incentive to you and your fellow sales reps. He says, "The first one of you with more than $10,000 in sales this week will win a weekend vacation for two at The Westin (including room, food, and entertainment) worth $1000!" Since your fifth wedding anniversary is fast approaching, you have a huge reason to achieve this goal. You have decided that YOU will be the winner. Your sales manager then hands you a blank GPC for ONE week only and you ask him how to fill it out and use it.

1. He explains the top half is for you to record what you actually DID. Write in the number of calls you made, demos you performed, and amount of sales you closed in the appropriate boxes for each day. These are your *Action and Progress Steps*, he explains. The gray columns are for you to keep a running total throughout the week for each Action and Progress Step. Every day and at the end of the week, you can easily tally the progress results you achieved along with the action you performed to get those results. He also explains that you can use the same format whether a goal is for two weeks, a month, or even longer. All you have to do is expand the size of the two tables (top half and bottom half).

6.4.41   Top half of GPC

Days of the Week	Calls	Totals	Demos	Totals	Sales	Totals
Monday						
Tuesday						
Wednesday						
Thursday						
Friday						
Saturday						
Sunday						
Totals						

2. Next your manager explains how to use the bottom half, which takes the numbers from the top half and creates an ongoing <u>picture</u> to show your progress. When used

correctly and updated daily, it becomes very easy to SEE if you are ahead of your goal, on track, or behind. Then you can quickly determine exactly which Action or Progress Step is at the root of the challenge and you can get instant coaching to help you fix whatever is wrong.

He explains you must first set your production goal and then work backward. You expect to win the contest, so you set your sales amount to be completed slightly higher than the incentive's requirement, because even if you fall a little behind, you will still surpass the required $10,000. *Refer to gray shaded area under Sales column in the following example (Section 6.4.42 Bottom half of GPC).*

You write $10,500 at the top of the Sales column because this is your total goal. You have seven days to complete this goal, and therefore you must sell $1,500 each day to reach your objective by the deadline. You start at the bottom of the column in the box on the right side and write in $1,500, which represents Day one's required production. Day 2 = $3,000. Your manager explains that your daily Progress Step for Monday is to sell $1,500 + $1,500 more for Tuesday, so at the end of the day on Tuesday, your sales volume is expected to be at $3,000 total. Day 3 = $4,500, and so on through Day 7. On the left side of the production, put the date corresponding to the total production expectation. Day one is Monday, November 12. Tuesday is the 13th, and so on. Now you have completed your Sales column, but in order to sell $1,500 each day you must do a certain number of demonstrations – an Action Step.

You calculate out of every five presentations you will close three for a total of $1,500, so your daily Action Step for presentations is five. On Day 2, your total demos should be 10, Day 3 = 15, and so on *(see gray shaded area under Demo column).* You do the same procedure for the date portion of the Demos column that you did for the Sales column.

Lastly, you determine that you will need to call upon 10 prospective customers each day in order to set up and do five demos for each day. Ten calls per day becomes your second and final Action Step. Using what you already know, you fill out the right side of the Calls column to visually track your performance *(see gray shaded area under Calls column)*. Finish the Calls column with the dates filled in correctly and now the bottom half of your GPC is ready for you to get started.

6.4.42   Bottom half of GPC

Calls		Demos		Sales	
70		**35**		**$10,500**	
11/18	70	11/18	35	11/18	$10,500
11/17	60	11/17	30	11/17	$9,000
11/16	50	11/16	25	11/16	$7,500
11/15	40	11/15	20	11/15	$6,000
11/14	30	11/14	15	11/14	$4,500
11/13	20	11/13	10	11/13	$3,000
11/12	10	11/12	5	11/12	$1,500

3.   Now your manager teaches you how to use the bottom portion of your GPC you have just created. He explains that you must use your **RED** marker to color in the date side of each column *every* day, no matter whether you take any action or produce any results that day or not. The point is the day will happen no matter what, whether you are productive or just sit on the couch and watch TV. You need to use red because if your red side is higher than your black side, it means something is wrong – your business is *"In-The-RED!"* You are behind

in your production, time is passing by faster than you are progressing, and you need to hurry up. Without the bottom half, the numbers on the top half would just remain numbers, thus NOT stir most people to take some immediate action to fix whatever is wrong. They would end the week confused and wonder what happened, but most would neither have a good answer nor be able to fix the problem the next week. They would struggle and maybe quit.

4. Next, your manager explains to color the right side, which represents what you actually DID (Action and Progress Steps), in **BLACK**. Do this late in the evening every day, after all possible results for that day have been achieved. When a business is *"In-The-BLACK"*, it means it is making money and doing well. When your black is even with your red, all is fine because you are exactly on track to achieve your goal by the deadline. When your black is higher than the red side, get excited because you are ahead of pace. You are on track to not just reach your goal but surpass it by the deadline. This could also mean you set your Action and/or Progress Steps too low and may need to raise them in future weeks to keep yourself excited to improve. Remember the goal must remain challenging yet still attainable.

5. Finally on your way out the door, your manager stresses that by using this GPC effectively, you will always know your exact position on your goal journey and be able to stay on track because you can easily evaluate your performance results and, if necessary, quickly change directions.

When I am focused on achieving something, I love coloring in my GPC. It is a part of my daily success routine whenever I am pushing to reach a goal. Because of my goal preparation and this simple tool, I typically achieve exactly what I set out to achieve. A GPC takes away the mystery and makes success systematic, which also makes it easy for you to duplicate no matter what the goal might be – business or personal. Developing this tool and using it effectively has without a doubt changed my life by giving me something I can apply whenever and for whatever I desire. Simply stated, it helps me remain self-motivated and get RESULTS!!!

One final point about this example is to emphasize the importance of having an accurate source of information to base your goal preparation upon. If you had a poor sales manager or coach who led you astray with wrong production expectations (i.e. average sale and average number of customers who schedule demos based upon calls), you could lose confidence because of continually not hitting goals that were based on unreasonable expectations. Do your best to make sure the numbers you depend upon to create your daily Action and Progress Steps are accurate and you are getting the necessary instruction from your coach to produce at the level they expect of you and you expect of yourself. To set unrealistic goals only sets us up for disappointment or even worse. Proper preparation is necessary to WIN!!!

6.5 Action

Through the process of creating your GPC, you have created daily Action and Progress Steps which must be achieved in order to reach your goal by the deadline you set. Immediate and small consistent action in a deliberate manner is key to success – bite-size pieces. However, action without thought is foolish, so do not act without your plan in place. Once it is ready get to work right away.

The natural law of inertia says that a body remains at rest or in a uniform motion in the same straight line unless acted upon by some external force. I have found that inertia is extremely powerful. If I have not been to the gym in awhile, I tend to just continue not going because it is what I have grown accustomed to. But the same law applies when I am **moving** in a specific focused direction, because I will eventually reach my destination. The critical word is MOVING. I have to get my body in motion, no matter how small the initial steps, in order to gradually develop momentum enough to keep moving. There is no more simpler answer to overcoming inertia than GET MOVING!

Samuel Johnson, an 18th century English poet, said "Nothing will ever be attempted if all possible objections must first be overcome." This is profound. You cannot overcome every objection in your mind before taking action or you will never act. Your mind can be your greatest asset or your worst enemy because, when allowed, your brain falls victim to the law of inertia and comes up with every excuse possible to stay stationary. However, Robert Collier, author of *The Secret of the Ages* in 1925, said "Take the first step, and your mind will mobilize all its forces to your aid. But the first essential is that you begin. Once the battle is started, all that is within and without you will come to your assistance ..." One of my favorite presidents, Franklin Delano Roosevelt, said it this way, "To reach a new port, we must sail – SAIL, not tie at anchor – **SAIL**, not drift." I quote these famous people who span more than 200 years because even though our world has undergone many amazing transformations during this time, the message sent through the ages from successful people is always the same – immediate, deliberate, consistent ACTION in a specific direction guarantees personal success. Once again, when you take action, victory becomes just a matter of time and effort.

Tomorrow will come and then the next day and so on. Before you know it a couple months will pass. When you start TODAY with your plan to achieve a specific goal, the same couple of months will still pass, but now when the months go by, you will have two months of progress behind you and the resulting confidence that progress brings. You will not want to stop moving forward because of inertia, which is now working for you, not against you. Progress feels good and you won't want to lose the ground you have fought so hard to win, so get off your tush and start. When necessary, start with absurdly easy steps because they will get you moving. Then gradually as you build momentum, you will expect more and more from yourself. I experience this every time I begin again to eat healthy and work out. I love to eat things that taste great but may not be the best for me. I cannot stand working out, so to get my overweight resting body and mind to begin to move initially takes great effort, but quickly becomes easier and easier. As it becomes easier, I will increase my workload and build momentum. Again, the most critical thing is to get started immediately!!!

When you are able to get up the courage to begin, you have the courage to succeed.
-David Viscott.

6.6 Tracking

You have set a goal, made a plan, and begun to take action, but how do you ensure you are on pace to achieve your goal by the deadline? How well did you follow your plan (daily success routine)? Every day you have certain Action and Progress Steps that must be achieved. Tracking is simply the documentation of your daily performance. What did you do? What were your results for that day's effort?

Numbers do not lie. Numbers have no emotion. Numbers are simple. Either you called 10 people, presented to five, and sold $1,500 today or not. Numbers are black and white, thus cannot be disputed. Tracking is accurate documentation of your numbers, which provides you the ability to evaluate your progress effectively and efficiently. Use your GPC or whatever other tool you create to keep track of your daily NUMBERS. The most important thing is that you keep accurate daily records of what you actually did and the results achieved.

Many years ago when I was selling for another company, I used a wall in my bedroom as my tracking tool. I would staple my copy of each order receipt right to the wall and then color my results on a paper thermometer I created. It was very simplistic but effective. I could clearly see every night before I went to sleep and morning when I got up how I was doing. I could not hide from my lack of performance when I was doing poorly. When I was doing well, it gave me great pride to see the wall being covered with pink order slips. My goal was to wallpaper the entire room with them and I eventually succeeded.

For me, out of sight is out of mind, so I could not allow my tracking tools to ever be out of sight. I needed them to be right in front of my face, or on my bedroom and bathroom walls, so I could keep myself focused at all times on what had to be done TODAY – my daily Action and Progress Steps. When I did not keep my tracking tools out in the open, or foolishly did not even make a GPC for a specific goal, or update my tools every day, it became too easy to ignore what I had to get done and to be lazy that day. We all have our own life-rhythms, emotional highs and lows, and I used to get lazy and hide during the lows, especially when I did not have a coach to help hold me accountable. I had a lot to accomplish and could not afford to waste precious time, so I needed to learn how to constantly remain at my most productive level, during a high or low period, whether I had a coach or not. This is why I created the entire Life GPA process and accompanying set of tracking and documentation tools (GPC, journal, and calendar). Track well and evaluation is a cinch.

6.7 Evaluation

Evaluation is the study of the tracked numbers. Goal time periods will affect how often I evaluate my performance, but I do so at least once a week. I learned a long time ago that when I would procrastinate until near the deadline to evaluate my progress, it usually ended up being too late to positively affect the outcome. For example, when I was in school and the teacher assigned a big project, most kids, myself included, would wait until the last possible minute to even begin working. Then we ended up pulling an all-nighter just to hand in a mediocre result. I became tired of not performing at my best, so I created tools to help keep me on pace.

When pursuing any goal, every weekend I would <u>honestly</u> evaluate my progress – good or bad. As long as I tracked myself closely, I would be able to quickly determine exactly what I was doing well or needed to improve. This allowed me to study to improve on my weaker areas before the next week even started. Good or bad results were both within my control. Close evaluation of my progress, or lack thereof, gave me a clear understanding of my current position. With this understanding, I was then able to change my direction (daily Action and Progress Steps) for the next week. If I was off track, I could quickly right the ship by increasing my performance in whichever area needed improvement.

When I did work closely with personal coaches, they were always impressed by my thorough understanding of my own strengths and weaknesses. This motivated them to want to help me do even better when times were good, and gave them the ability to focus in like a laser beam on my areas that needed to be improved. There was little guesswork so I was able to get the exact coaching I needed in the shortest amount of time. This process increased my immediate productivity and long-term momentum.

6.7.1 Making your spouse happy

For the following two examples of daily Action and Progress Step evaluation, we will return to the Weekend Getaway sales contest which you decided to win to celebrate your fifth wedding anniversary.

Example one – You are two days into the contest and have made a total of 30 calls, 8 demonstrations, and 5 sales for a total of $2,000. The top half of your GPC is straightforward documentation of your performance, but the bottom half is actually interesting. You are ahead of your *Calls* Action Step by a full day, but behind by 2 demonstrations on your *Demos* Action Step. As a result of your actions, your *Sales* Progress Step is down by $1,000, which inspires lots of urgency to find out how to fix what's wrong, so you call your manager and schedule some one-on-one time.

Days of the Week	Calls	Totals	Demos		Totals		Sales	Totals
Monday	15	15	3	(2)	3	(2)	$1000	$1000
Tuesday	15	30	5	(3)	8	(5)	$1000	$2000
Wednesday								
Thursday								
Friday								
Saturday								
Sunday								
Totals								

Calls			Demos			Sales	
70			**35**			**$10,500**	
11/18	70		11/18	35		11/18	$10,500
11/17	60		11/17	30		11/17	$9,000
11/16	50		11/16	25		11/16	$7,500
11/15	40		11/15	20		11/15	$6,000
11/14	30		11/14	15		11/14	$4,500
11/13	20		11/13	10		11/13	$3,000
11/12	10		11/12	5		11/12	$1,500

When you walk in for your meeting, you feel upset because you believe you have not done as much as you should have.

Surprisingly, the first thing your coach does is compliment you on what you DID achieve – you called more people than your daily goal required and also made your first sale! This positive recognition changes your whole attitude and you smile, then ask him to help you improve. He says, "Yesterday's lack of performance is in the past. Can you change what you did not do?" You say, "No." Then he stresses to let it go, "Your past does not control your future unless you permit it to. Let's study your performance together, learn from it, and strategically plan how you will improve when you go back to work."

After looking at your GPC, both of you determine you need a little more coaching on how to overcome excuses over the phone, so you can set up more demos. Right now you are only 27-percent (8 demos for 30 calls), not the 50-percent level you should be at. In addition, he asks you about the specific face-to-face sales objections customers have given you, which you must have struggled with because you only averaged $400 per sale instead of the $500 expected of you. You and your coach proceed to role-play back and forth. He teaches you again what to say and do and you practice it right in front of him.

After only an hour, you feel polished and ready to go back in the field. You run out of the office refreshed and excited once again. A few hours ago you were concerned you might not be able to succeed at sales. You thought maybe this just wasn't right for you, but now, with the help of your coach, your excitement is restored and confidence is once again building. You feel good about what you did correctly, understand what went wrong, and are jazzed to do better the next time.

Your manager made a specific statement you will always remember as you develop your leadership skills – EXCITED PEOPLE PRODUCE! A leader must keep the team excitedly focused upon achievement and believing in themselves, which will result in better production and better lives for all producing team members. As you drive off, you conclude your manager must be a master mechanic. In only an hour he was able to clean your vehicle's windshield by refreshing your focus on the prize (reason for achieving the goal), recharge your battery with emotional energy (someone believes you CAN do it), and help you learn and practice how to produce better by reviewing your vehicle's owner's manual (nuts-and-bolts, how-to information).

Example two – Now you are four days in and you have spoken to your manager multiple times. Another salesperson has almost won the contest already, so you turn up the heat. At the end of day four you have made a total of 50 calls, 21 demonstrations, and 13 sales for a total of $11,500. You just made your last sale of $2,000 which pushed you over the required $10,000, so now you rush to the office to show your coach and claim your prize, assuming you are the first one done.

Days of the Week	Calls	Totals	Demos		Totals		Sales	Totals
Monday	15	15	3	(2)	3	(2)	$1000	$1000
Tuesday	15	30	5	(3)	8	(5)	$1000	$2000
Wednesday	10	40	8	(5)	16	(10)	$5000	$7000
Thursday	10	50	5	(3)	21	(13)	$4500	$11,500
Friday								
Saturday								
Sunday								
Totals								

Calls	
70	
11/18	70
11/17	60
11/16	50
11/15	40
11/14	30
11/13	20
11/12	10

Demos	
35	
11/18	35
11/17	30
11/16	25
11/15	20
11/14	15
11/13	10
11/12	5

Sales	
$10,500	
11/18	$10,500
11/17	$9,000
11/16	$7,500
11/15	$6,000
11/14	$4,500
11/13	$3,000
11/12	$1,500

When you walk into the office, the first thing your manager wants to see is your GPC. You attempt to hand him the orders but he wants to see all of your performance details. A good coach is not just looking for the money but searching for as many ways as possible to train his team members to improve. Finally, he accepts your orders and congratulates you on successfully being the first person with MORE THAN $10,000. Right as the confetti and balloons fall from the ceiling your nemesis walks in with his sales, but you won because you were the first! Because of your performance, accurate tracking, regular evaluation, and good coaching, you successfully achieved your goal and *you and your spouse live happily ever after. The end!*

6.8   Change

The only absolute in life is change. After evaluation, change your daily Action and Progress Steps when necessary. Increase what you must DO and/or PRODUCE but never change either the deadline or the goal. As the deadline approaches, the pace appears to quicken. This feeling is what I call your *Sense Of Urgency.* When I am working on achieving a goal and my deadline is closing in, the people around me know it. I tend to become even more impatient, aggressive, tunnel-minded, pushy, demanding, focused, and strategic than normal. Obtaining what I set out to do by the deadline I set for myself is an absolute necessity. Excuses and distractions are ever present, but I cannot allow myself to give in and lose my focus. Failure is unacceptable – it is just not an option.

Because I invest such a great deal of effort into properly preparing my goal and creating my plan, I know I can accomplish it so long as I follow my success routine. My toughest competition is myself. To give your best and later be able to surpass your own best is the perfect reason for a reward. I tend to be my own biggest critic, which is how I believe it should be, so long as I don't just beat myself up and drag down my excitement level. I seek to give myself ONLY constructive criticism that

I can learn from. Honesty is the best policy – if you were lazy, then admit it and go on. If you need help in some area, seek out the proper guidance, learn, adapt, and move on. There is no reason to fear change because personal growth cannot occur without change and any increase in income must be preceded by a moment of personal growth. Enjoying my lifestyle involves constant personal development which requires perpetual change and personal growth.

6.9   Reward

Reward Points are necessary off ramps and rest stops on your Path of Performance. When I was much younger, I made the same mistake many people seem to make. I set myself up for failure without even realizing it. I would reward myself *only* after I had done something extraordinary. The time periods between rewards was often so long that I became burned out and never reached the finish line. This used to frustrate me beyond belief. Then, I amplified the mistake by beating myself up over my loss. It was a vicious circle of unfulfilled goals and depression. Sometimes I even questioned whether I would ever be a success. Fortunately, I wised up and started treating myself better.

When I moved to Denver, Colorado in 1997, I had specific goals to accomplish and an absolute 11-week deadline. I had multiple GPCs because I had both personal and business objectives to reach. After feeling the sting of burnout, I learned to reward myself more often, ideally once a week, with something small but worthwhile. I would align the reward with my evaluation, not that I needed a formal evaluation to know whether I was going to reward myself or not. Trust me; I knew my numbers in my head and on my GPC *every* day. I colored my chart and made a strategy for what I needed to *do* every single day in order to achieve my goal for the week. It may seem silly, but when I was in Denver my reward was to *allow* myself to go to a local restaurant called Perkins and purchase my favorite bread bowl salad. I loved this thing – Teriyaki chicken breast with bleu cheese dressing, hold the chives. At about 10 p.m., after I was finished working, I would go over to pick my salad up every Friday night. Then I would savor every bite because I had worked hard and produced well to earn this treat. As I have already stated, I produce greater business results when I also implement a strict physical fitness routine. It clears my head of the emotional cobwebs and keeps me on track. So within my 11 weeks in Denver, I got in great shape, made a lot of money, and rewarded myself each week with a simple, great-tasting salad.

Reward often but be strict on yourself. The reward must be earned. Don't let yourself accept close as good enough to get a reward. Make yourself suffer if you fall short, even if you are extremely close. Close only counts in kissing and hand grenades. Life only pays on results. Therefore I only pay myself when I produce – no exceptions. I have found when it comes to motivating people there are two schools of thought. One group endorses using a stick to drive someone. This is what I call negative motivation. It works, but only for short bursts of energy and time and often creates resentment between leader and team member. Negative motivation is when someone says, "Do _____ or else _____ will happen!" An example of this would be if your boss at a J.O.B. says, "Either you come in and work on your weekend off, or I won't approve that vacation you have requested for next month." I usually see negative motivators use this tool to control. Often these are dictators who are on a power trip and get excited by embarrassing, controlling, or demeaning others. I don't care for this kind of motivation. It is NOT what I practice most of the time, but has its place and works well in extreme situations when extreme measures are needed to produce results.

I prefer to use the carrot or positive to motivate. "Do _____ and you will get _____!" I use this method most of the time because I know I will work harder to achieve a reward than avoid a punishment. When somebody tries to punish me, even if I am trying to do it to myself, I develop a "go to hell" attitude. My grandmother told me often, "Allen, you will catch more flies with honey than with vinegar." This statement is true, not just because honey is stickier but is sweeter than vinegar. People love to strive to achieve and earn something. When I lead people, including myself, I seek to understand what that person needs (why they do what they do), then set them up in a position to earn whatever they desire. I neither have the desire nor the patience to control other people – it is just too much work. I did not get into business to have a professional career in Adult Babysitting. Instead, I seek to desheepitize them by teaching them what they need to do by a certain date and then coach them on the best methods of achieving the objective.

I seek to give people accurate tools to help them help themselves. Ultimately a person needs to be responsible to motivate themselves – it is THEIR life after all. All real motivation comes from inside the person, anyway. So I study them looking for the right hot-button to sweeten the deal, which gives them a reward to strive to obtain. Build into your Success Routine regular and specific Reward Points which are appropriate for the work you will do to earn them. When you start something brand new, such as getting yourself back into the gym, set Reward Points closer together in the beginning to slowly begin to build the necessary momentum. As you see improvement, gradually make the rewards better but further apart. For example, allow yourself a daily cheat treat in the beginning. As you start to see results only allow a cheat meal once a week. You must constantly keep challenging and enticing yourself or you risk getting burned out or bored. Either way you risk losing your momentum by allowing friction to slow you down.

Most of us strange people who chose to swim upstream against the current need only a bit of praise or encouragement now and then to keep going. Treat yourself well. When you have earned it, take an off ramp, rest a while, and enjoy the fruits of your labor now and then. Life is too short to work *all* of the time. Savor your victories frequently because it *will* inspire you to have more of them even more often. Beat yourself up and you may just get tired of attempting at all, which would really be a shame. Set yourself up to win!

6.10 Record

I purchased my first journal in 1990 and I have been keeping them ever since. The one I use exclusively is the red hardcover journal made by "AT-A-GLANCE," which is sold at office supply stores. I buy one book for each year EVERY year without fail. My belief originally was to simply document what I learned, observed, experienced, etc. I would write as much as possible on both good and bad so I could be proactive for the future. I was leveraging my current success so I had it right there to refer to if necessary.

Many times since I began keeping a journal I became stuck or struggled with a specific issue. Then I remembered dealing with this issue before, so I pulled out my old journal and looked up the information. It was easy to see what I had done in the past to fix this same issue. Then I applied the information and like magic, overcame my challenge. Productivity has been a common theme throughout this book and here it is again. Rich people understand that time and emotional energy equal money and to waste either repeating the same mistakes is stupid. Do it one time, learn from it, document exactly what you did, and then keep it as a reference tool for the future. It does not matter whether it is personal or business, the same issues seem to come up again and again. Expect them and prepare for them so you have little if any non-productive time or wasted emotional energy.

This was the reason I started keeping a journal. Eighteen years later I have a library full of documented successes and failures, which is a priceless gift to give someone who would treasure such a thing. Intelligence is to learn from your own mistakes, but wisdom is to learn from other people's mistakes so you do not even make them. I want to help my sons be wise and not have to suffer from the same stupid mistakes I have made. When the time is right, my boys will each get a copy of dad's journals to do with as they wish. They can read about the highs and lows and better understand and appreciate the toil that went into creating the lifestyle we enjoy, so they won't take it for granted. I believe that if a life is worth living, it is worth recording!

6.11 A real-life example of using the Success Formula to achieve Victory

In October 2003 I was on a business trip to Baltimore. I was still hobbling around on crutches from a motorcycle accident I had in July, in which I injured my ankle and had doctors screw it back together. I had zero intention of taking on a Body Fat (BF) loss competition, but that quickly changed. An overly confident young man whom I will call Bob was going through training in a business I owned. When I visited the office where he was training that day, Bob made a smart-mouthed remark about how I was always eating healthy but never seemed to appear to lose any weight. I took this as a personal challenge from Bob and told him to put his money where it his mouth was, and he agreed.

The contest was relatively simple. Two overly competitive guys with big egos, who both needed to get in shape, challenged each other to see who could change his body the most by a specific date. What was at stake was $5,000, a shaved head and eyebrows, and most important, bragging rights FOREVER!

6.11.1 Terms

We agreed upon the following terms and drew up a contract. We strove to make everything as fair and accurate as possible so there would not be a sore loser whining about anything. For a competitive person like myself, there is nothing more irritating in a competition than unclear rules and boundaries. Other than what we agreed to in our contract, barring the cutting off of a limb, we agreed *"anything goes."*

1. <u>Formula.</u> First Bob and I agreed upon the formula used to calculate the winner. The only fair way to compete was to base the winner on who actually changed his body the most and we came up with the following formula.

    Starting BF percent minus Ending BF percent = BF percent Drop

    BF percent Drop divided by Starting BF percent = Overall BF percent of Change

    This way if a guy who had 10 percent BF competed against a guy who had 30 percent BF, the contest would be fair, because it would be much easier for the bigger guy to drop 5 percent than the thinner guy.

2. <u>Deadline.</u> The contest began on 10/28/2003 and ended 3/2/2004.

3. <u>Baseline.</u> We needed to know EXACTLY what our starting BF percent was so we could determine a clear winner without debate or argument. I learned that the most accurate way to measure BF was by hydro-testing. Basically, you strip naked, sit on a metal chair, get lowered into a small tank of water, exhale every ounce of air in your lungs, hold yourself under water for 5-10 seconds,

then raise your head and gasp for breath while trying not to inhale any water. Repeat this process 4 times and the computer gives you a very accurate BF percentage reading. The closest place I found for us to do this was at the University of Maryland.

Here is where we started.

	Me	**Bob**
Total pounds of body weight	224.4	195.1
Total pounds of lean weight	169.4	118.5
Total pounds of body fat	55.00	76.6
Age	33	23
Height (inches)	72	70
Starting BF percent	24.52	39.27

4. Final Measurement. We agreed to fly to Baltimore and have the exact same BF test done by the same guy at the same place. Bob and I wanted to leave no possible dispute point. Everything was to be by the book.

6.11.2 The Process

March 2nd seemed a long way off but I knew it would come quickly. I flew back to Minnesota and immediately asked my orthopedic surgeon to remove my cast and examine my ankle. I needed to be cleared to begin doing cardio. It was an agonizing 10-day wait until my appointment because I knew who I was up against. I will paint a mental picture of Bob for you. If Bob was in a cross-country meet and got his foot stuck in a bear trap out in the woods, he would gnaw his own leg off and hobble across the finish line on his bloody stump. So even though I could not begin exercising yet, I used those 10 days to do my goal preparation, research, and planning. I spent 10 days preparing to win, before I was even able to begin to take any Action Steps to achieve any Progress Steps.

When I saw the doctor, he told me to wait another two weeks before starting to jog and even later to run. No way did I plan on listening to him. "Doctors are always too cautious anyway," I told myself, so I pushed it and started jogging lightly that same day. I felt a great sense of urgency because I needed to win.

Here is what I learned and did to prepare.

1. Because of working with trainers in the past, especially Zoltan in Miami, I was familiar with the basics of losing BF while still gaining lean mass. However, I needed to get <u>exact</u> data in order to prepare a challenging yet attainable finish BF percentage to shoot for as my goal. I had to calculate the specific Ending percentage I would need in order to win. This was tough because Bob lived nowhere near Minnesota, so I did not have any idea how hard he was working out, what he was eating, or how he was going to train. So there was some guesswork, but the majority of my information was based upon accurate scientific facts of how the human body works. I took everything I knew and created a chart on which I could track, with some certainty, what I anticipated Bob's BF percent loss was at any given time. Looking at this often kept me focused when I wanted to eat a pizza or avoid the gym. I decided I could not afford to lose – period. Failure was never an option.

2. I went online and researched healthy methods of losing weight. I already knew that a pound of BF = 3,500 calories and losing BF is all about caloric deficit (burn more than you consume). If you burn 500 more calories each day than you consume, you should lose one pound of actual BF per week.

3. I calculated both Bob's and my Basal Metabolic Rate

(BMR), which told me how many calories we would burn by doing nothing all day. Then I had to make assumptions based on how hard I thought he would train and how healthily he would eat. I learned long ago that there is NO magic pill or machine for losing weight. A huge industry has been built upon giving people false hope for the *secret potion*, but no such thing exists. I made my best guess of where Bob would finish on March 2, 2004 and I ended up pretty close. Then I calculated where I would HAVE to finish in order to beat him convincingly.

4. My personal goal was to end up at 9 percent BF, which would have been a 63 percent overall change. I determined there was no way under the sun Bob would do better than a 63 percent change, so that became my target.

5. After all the research and calculating, the plan (Success Routine) I came up with was pretty simple and I began to create my 100-day GPC (14 weeks). I started my GPC on 11/24/03 because it was exactly 100 days out from our deadline and it gave me a little more time to allow my ankle to strengthen.

6. My two Progress Points were BF percent and Scale Weight. With these two measurements I could evaluate my actual progress and make changes if necessary to my Action Steps.

    BF percent Progress Point. In order to reach my goal by the deadline, I calculated I had to lose 0.14 percent BF per day.

    Scale Weight Progress Point. Each day I had to lose 0.3 pounds. I weighed myself every day at the exact same time using the same scale. I realized Scale Weight was very deceptive but it was really the only easily accessible in-house measuring tool I had.

As long as I stayed on track, I would end the contest on 3/2/04 weighing 198 pounds and having only 9 percent BF.

7. My three Action Points were Weight Training, Cardio, and Diet. I could control these three things completely. I chose whether to eat right and go to the gym. I figured my BMR to be 1,967, which meant I would burn 1,967 calories if I did absolutely nothing during the day. However, I calculated that with my daily Action Steps I would burn a total of 2,951 calories every single day. I slightly underestimated the 2,951 as well, thereby building another safety cushion into my plan. Even though I developed a great plan for victory, 100 days is a long time to stay 100 percent perfect, so I had to have a little bit of fudge room.

Weight Training Action Point. I had to <u>lift weights five days per week</u> in order to burn the necessary number of calories to reach my goal. I figured I would burn 400 calories during every weight training hour as long as I pushed myself. This is why I hired Amara, a very good trainer in Minneapolis, who lived what he preached. I was working with someone I believed in and I felt accountable to show up every day. The 400-calorie assumption was conservative as well because when done correctly, along with proper diet and supplementation, weight training will add lean muscle mass. Adding muscle to your body is just like adding horsepower to your vehicle's engine; more muscle burns more calories. The end result is increasing my *momentum* of calorie burning.

Cardio Action Point. I required myself to do <u>30 minutes of cardio every single day</u> for 100 consecutive days. According to my calculations, if I kept my heart rate at the optimal level, I would burn 10 calories per minute doing cardio. I bought and constantly wore a heart monitor while jogging on the treadmill to maximize my efficiency. I often ran outside on the highway near my home because I knew that running in 30-degree weather would burn even more calories than normal cardio, just like drinking ice water will burn more calories than room-temperature water. I knew who I was competing against and the chips were stacked against me because I was older and injured. I had to maximize every possible thing I could in order to win.

Diet Action Point. My diet would be limited to a strict intake of <u>1,896 calories per day</u>, thereby creating a deficit of 1,055 calories per day. Multiply the 1,055 times seven days and I would burn a total of 7,385 more calories each week than I consumed, which would result in 2.1 pounds of BF burned each week. Over my goal time period, I would finish exactly where I planned to. I also learned that when a person burns BF, he typically burns up some muscle tissue as well. I wanted to avoid this as much as possible, so I structured my diet to feed my muscles with plenty of protein and restricted the bad fats and simple carbs. My daily diet consisted of 103 grams of carbs, 258 of protein, and 45 of fats. This even allowed a 47-calorie per day cushion just in case I got one of those intense sugar cravings. My focus was on quality, clean foods, so I even went so far as charting exactly what foods I needed to eat at each meal and how many meals per day. I put this information into a spreadsheet and printed out a copy for each day. All I had to do was look at my paper plan for that day, follow it exactly, and over time my goal would be realized. I left nothing to chance.

With all of this information, I created my GPC and daily Success Routine. My GPC had five columns and took two pieces of paper which I taped together – it was big and complicated-looking but really was in essence very simple. Each Action and Progress Step got its own column, so every day I could color it in using red and black markers. I would get up every day at 5 a.m., go to the gym and do whatever was required for that day's exercise, eat exactly what I was supposed to eat, weigh myself, and every other week I got a hydro-test done at the University of St. Thomas in Minnesota to track my actual progress. I faithfully colored in my GPC every day and every single weekend sat down and evaluated my progress. I kept the plan exactly the same until the final 30 days. Then I compared where I thought Bob was at and looked at my level of progress and was unhappy. In order to win, I needed to become even more disciplined and work even harder. I could not let Bob win, no matter what!

6.11.3 Final Month

I cut my daily caloric intake to only 1,473 total calories (94 carbs, 218 protein, and 25 fats) and did not allow myself to have any kind of *cheat meals* or snacks. I broke this up into 6 meals to keep my body working in overdrive all day. It gradually got harder to focus and think because a person's brain needs a certain amount of fat to function and mine was struggling. I was tired most of the time because the only energy my body really had to burn was my fat stores. All of the carbs I consumed were complex carbs, which made my body work harder to process them. I eliminated all sources of sodium because I figured that water retention could cause as much as a half of a percent of additional BF to show on the final test. However, I kept my protein consumption high because I wanted my body to burn dietary protein rather than digesting the muscle tissue I had worked so hard to build.

	WEIGHT TRAINING		CARDIO		Actual		DIET		WEIGHT		Actual		BODYFAT %		% CH
	3/2	TEST	3/2	ST			3/2	TEST	3/2	TEST			3/2	TEST	
0						30									
1					OFF	29				205.9	TRAVEL				44%
2					45/RR					206.3	TRAVEL				43%
3					30/RR	27				206.6	TRAVEL				43%
4					OFF	26					TRAVEL				42%
5					OFF	25					208.0				41%
6					30/40						208.5				41%
7					30/43						207.5				40%
8					15/BK	22					209.0				39%
9					120/RR	21					216.5				38%
10					OFF	20					209.5				38%
11					30/434						210.5				37%
12					45/313						211.0				36%
13					30/48						213.0				36%
14					60/RR						214.0				35%
15					45/648						214.0				34%
16					NONE						215.5				33%
17					45/706						214.0				33%
18					67/1002						212.5				32%
19					45/673						213.5				31%
20					45/648						215.5				31%
21					45/582						216.5				30%
22					NONE						220.5				29%
23					NONE						?				28%
24					30/RR						?				28%
25					30/40						216.5				27%
26					45/RR						215.0				26%
27					30/296						214.5				25%
28					30/431						214.0				25%
29					30/452						215.5				24%
30					START						216.5				23%

1473

10/28 224.4   10/28 24.52488%

☆ = 100% Perfect Diet   ✓ = Oil   - = Pool

6.11.4 The End

On March 2nd, I was ready to have this competition over. Bob and I met in Baltimore and I was happy to have pushed myself so hard. He looked skinny! I joked with him when we started this crazy competition by calling him a walking pat of butter, but he did not look like that anymore. He had trained to be a boxer during this time and his coach had pushed him to be ready to actually walk into a real boxing ring and compete. Together we drove to the University of Maryland, met Matt again, and did our test.

Here are the results.

	Me	**Bob**
Starting BF percent	24.52	39.27
Ending BF percent	13.67	23.36
BF Percent Drop	10.85	15.91
Overall BF percent of Change	44.24	40.51

Right after the BF test was done, Bob and I sat down at Wendy's and ate a triple cheeseburger, fries, and I had some Krispy Kreme doughnuts to celebrate my victory. This contest was an amazing personal journey, but not something I was willing to maintain forever. I learned a lot and gained an incredible amount of experience from which I will draw to maintain a healthier way of life forever.

I admit I built Bob up in my mind to be a tougher competitor than he really was in order to motivate myself to push harder during my off moments and *stay the course*. Ultimately, I won and this proved to me once again anything is possible when you implement the Success Formula. There isn't any magic. The Success Formula is just a process, a different way of thinking, but thinking is what separates the millionaire from the bum on the street. It does not matter whether your ideal lifestyle requires money, possessions, or physical health; all of your dreams are within your reach. Just break the dreams into goals, the goals into bite-size pieces, and then achieve them one by one. Before you know it, you will be enjoying a lifestyle while others just continue to earn a living.

6.12   Truth # 6 Action Points

Life GPA is a crucial part of your own personal formula for success. By improving your Life GPA, you will increase your confidence, and when you gain the necessary mental momentum to prevent the opposing forces from stopping you, you are assured to live every day the lifestyle you desire. How can you ensure you will achieve everything you set out to?

A.   Set your **G**oal. Decide upon your goal, one single step to accomplish on your ultimate climb toward a personal dream. Define it clearly in the form of numbers to be achieved. It must be both challenging yet remain attainable. A great goal will force you to stretch slightly further than you have done before, thus forcing you to grow. Create a *Sense of Urgency* by understanding clearly WHY you will achieve this goal and assigning a fixed-in-stone deadline. Commit your goal to paper and tell every supportive person who will hold you accountable what you WILL accomplish and by when.

B.   Develop your **P**lan. This is the map showing both your destination and the best route to take to make the journey. Take your goal, break it down into bite-size pieces (Action and Progress Steps) for every single day, and from these steps develop your personal Success Routine. Create a GPC or similar tool to track the progress of your routine and update it daily. Every week evaluate your results; remain flexible enough to change your daily Action and/ or Progress Steps to ensure your goal is accomplished by the deadline. Don't forget to treat yourself well – build it into your plan. Set Reward Points.

C.   Take **A**ction. Accomplish exactly what your daily Success Routine requires – no excuses. Before you go to bed ask yourself this question, "Did I do everything possible to achieve my objective for today?" If you answer YES, then sleep well and hit it hard again tomorrow. If you answer NO, get back to work to figure out what went wrong. Make any necessary adjustments to your routine for tomorrow so you can make up for your lack of production from today. Leverage your current success and ensure you don't make the same mistakes again, by recording for your future what you learned and accomplished today. Your records will be an amazing resource to refer back to and reflect upon concerning your personal growth and maturation.

STEP 2

Where Are You Now?
Summation of Action Points

Truth # 4

To get there,
first you must know your starting position.

A. Decide which type of vehicle you will use to get to your desired destination.

B. Know your current financial starting point exactly.

C. Pack appropriately and get started.

Truth # 5

Where you will end up,
depends a lot upon who travels with you.

A. Get yourself in the right environment.

B. Build your teams.

C. Make your life a career in People Studies.

Truth # 6

The higher your Life GPA,
the more enjoyable your lifestyle.

A. Set your **G**oal.

B. Develop your **P**lan.

C. Take **A**ction.

In order to boldly travel into the unknown we must have a sense of where we are headed. What will give us a fulfilling life? You cannot afford to allow fear or a lack of self-discipline to slow you down. Only those who simply will not quit will win at the game of life.

Use the information within the next three Truths to choose your path and travel efficiently in style.

TRUTH # 7

Success in life is a journey, NOT a destination.

7.1 Which path will you choose?

In life I believe there are only two paths to choose from. The first is the *Path of Excuses*. I see this path as an eight-lane freeway going in one direction, to a town called Regretsville. The road is well lit. Lots of people you know are pretending to happily travel this path, and they are waving their arms for you to come and join them. Deep down they know they have settled for mediocrity and are miserable but misery loves company, so the herd again beckons for you to join. The freeway is jam-packed with traffic. There are many wonderful vendors on the side of the road offering great deals to borrow their money to buy all kinds of new flashy junk, which you just have to buy. They entice you in with free stuff. All you have to do is just sign up for their credit cards and loans. This path looks like a carnival on the surface, deceptively so. Once you give in and take this path, you're stuck. Like a moth to the bug-zapper, you got caught by the façade and didn't even notice the 12-foot electrified fence surrounding the freeway. Now it is too late. The escape door is locked and guarded. You are trapped in the rat race. Like all your friends living in Regretsville, you settle into your J.O.B., continue to use other people's money to buy what you *must have*, and spend the rest of your life in debt working to make other people rich until they don't need you any longer. You no longer own your productivity because you traded it for a few shiny beads and trinkets. What looked so inviting has turned into a living hell. Whenever you try to escape, the other crabs just grab on and pull you right back into the bucket.

Every day of your life, you suffer the worst pain of all – the pain of regret. You regret not having worked harder to get that college degree, or to break free from your J.O.B., you regret surrounding yourself with other sheeple just so you didn't feel like such a failure. Whenever anyone else attempts to break out of this self-imposed prison, you now even find yourself scorning them for being different. You curse them for thinking they are better than you. But secretly you know the truth. You don't want to see them succeed because that will be a daily reminder of what you have not done with your life and how you accepted losing as a habit.

Over time you become numb, cynical, and close your mind off to what might have been, if only you made a different choice. It is easy to shut down. You tell yourself, "Everything is really OK, not great, but not too bad, either." Your employer and the government are happy to keep you as part of the herd. They make it as comfortable here as possible so you really don't try to escape anymore. Your spirit is eventually broken, like the elephant that only needs to be tied with a weak rope instead of a strong chain once it has given up and accepted its existence in captivity. A loser at the game of life, you eventually go to your grave with little more than unfulfilled hopes, ideas, and dreams. You have become just another memory of a warning of what not to do.

Is this YOUR ideal lifestyle?

Will this be YOUR typical way of life?

It is YOUR choice, after all!

The second path is performance. The Path of Performance has pain too, LOTS of it, but the pain here immediately begins to go away and quickly becomes a distant memory as your rewards are realized. Think of the Olympic athlete. When they are standing on top of the world receiving their gold medal, do you honestly believe they are thinking about all of the thousands of miles they have run? Or the tens of thousands of pounds they have lifted in the weight room? Of course not! They are far too overwhelmed feeling victorious to be concerned with what it took to get there. For them, it always was the passionate pursuit of the victory that mattered most, not the toil along the way. I have heard that a brave man dies but once and the coward dies a thousand times. The cowards die every single day. They regret over and over what they have not done and the decisions they did not make. Life hands out victories only to those who perform!

The Path of Performance is like climbing Mt. Everest during a blizzard at night. You struggle to breathe because the oxygen is thin. Your lungs scream "STOP!" but you keep on. The frostbite begins to attack your nose, fingertips and toes – but you push on. You cannot even feel your legs. Pain would even become a welcome friend as you are now numb from the bone-chilling cold – but you don't care. You feel alone, at times frightened as your mind occasionally wanders. Suddenly you feel a jerk from a rope tied to your waist and then notice the faint set of footprints ahead of you in the snow. You are not alone! Someone has been here before you and they are leading the way – your coach.

WHAM! Out from behind a rock you passed comes a whack on your head and you feel blood trickle down the back of your neck.

Suddenly you realize it was someone you trusted and thought was on your side, but that person just smacked you in the head with a club. You stumble, drop to one knee, but the little voice inside your head says you must push on! "Get up!" it screams. You slowly begin to move forward and upward once again, one step at a time. Lift your left leg, place your foot, adjust your weight, do it again with the right leg, hold on, "You can DO this," the voice says, "I must do this," you chant to yourself. On and on you climb, one step at a time. When the storm lightens, you get a glimpse of the world from 29,029 feet and it looks good. Only the few who chose to live, to fight instead of settle, have ever seen this view. Some gave up at base camp but most never even attempted to reach the mountain. You have crested Everest. You are a winner and NOBODY can ever take that away from you – NOBODY!!!

Yes, there is pain on the Path of Performance – a lot of it. But pain is an undeniable part of life. Which pain will you choose to endure? The everlasting relentless pain of regret or the momentary pain of performance? Life only pays on results, not talk. Second place is just the first loser. So find a way to win, keep going, and never give up on yourself! When you decide to never settle for second place, *life has but only one option – to pay you the lifestyle you demand!.*

7.2   Keep between the lines

In order to live on the Path of Performance, to become the best you can be, to have everything you could possibly desire, I have learned some very important rules to live by.

1.   <u>Comfort Zone.</u> The opposite of successful is comfortable. Whenever I am too comfortable, I end up driving my vehicle right into the ditch. It never seems to fail. Personal growth does not occur within our Comfort

Zone. When you are comfortable, you are not striving or pushing yourself. When you are no longer growing, you start dying. This is the exact reason I have lived in so many locations over the years. Fortunately, with my skill in sales, ability to manage a business well, and my leadership capabilities, I have been able to go wherever I wanted whenever I got the urge to go. I have developed the ability to feel when I am becoming too sedentary and need a change. Then I will relocate temporarily to further my study of people-patterns in a new area. Why have I done this? As a result of relocating, I kept myself sharp in my people studies career because so much in a different city is new, unfamiliar, and exciting. I will intensify the experience by doing new and different things whenever I think of them. This is why I have gone skydiving, sailing, scuba diving, taken a flying lesson and so much more, all in an effort to keep myself out of my Comfort Zone and constantly growing. I seek to maximize my productivity and results and I am unable to do this while sitting in a nice office in my hometown. What works for me does not have to be exactly the same for you. Just keep yourself on your toes using whatever uncomfortable process you need. Hire a personal trainer to push you out of your comfort zone, learn to dance or sing. It does not matter *what* exactly, just that it is new, exciting, and forces you to stretch yourself.

2. Big Rewards. What dream possessions or experiences do you have in mind for your life? I have yearned to build and live in a log cabin mansion since I was a little boy. I have the perfect piece of property already and will begin to build in the upcoming years. Maybe you want to own a Ferrari, catch a 500-pound marlin, dive on a sunken ship, buy a $1,000,000 yacht to sail around the world, win an ultimate fighting match, or organize a dogsled run across Antarctica. Whatever you can dream, you can

achieve. You only have to build yourself, your resources, and your success teams and then pull the trigger.

Create a life timeline and chart out what you want and when you plan to have it. Let your spouse and life coach know all about what you expect to do during your life. Gradually take steps toward these objectives as you become stronger. Use the same Success Formula I gave you but extend it over much longer periods of time. You still decide upon it, visualize it, set the goal, make the plan, create a deadline, track yourself, evaluate, enjoy regular smaller rewards, and record it. Whatever you want, the process to obtain it is the same, just bigger! So take the time to dream, put your milestone markers on your life chart, and then set out to climb each and every mountain.

3.   Patience. This is a funny word for me. I seem to have built a reputation for being one of the most impatient people you would ever meet. I live by the belief that the only good things coming to those who wait is whatever is left behind by those who hustled and got there first. I still believe hustling is important but I am gradually beginning to understand the value of patience, especially as a father. Life has many wonderful things for us to savor. You would not want to just guzzle a fine wine. You should smell it, sip it, and drink in the experience. Life will happen fast enough.

You must mentally be where you are 100 percent no matter where you are. Many people I have met are dreaming of their vacation while at work and are not nearly as productive as they could have been. When they are on vacation the guilt sets in and they cannot stop thinking about work. Control over one's mindset is at the heart of enjoying your ideal lifestyle. Because I was productive when I worked, I am able to play. When my son has a baseball game, I will be there. I watched every single testing and sparring tournament my wife had as she climbed to her third-degree black belt. By patience, I mean drink in the experiences of life, work when you must, but play as much as you can and be careful not to rush the good stuff.

4. <u>Be "Strange."</u> As you move down the Path of Performance and your lifestyle dreams materialize before your eyes, don't make the mistake that I did through much of my twenties. I built businesses, made money, and had some great moments, but I should have taken more time to dance, yell, give gifts for no reason, hug those I met instead of give a handshake, and kiss as many babies as possible. Fortunately I did learn this next point in my early twenties – Do NOT apologize for living your life the way you want! If I step on your foot, I will say I'm sorry. But I have found that to apologize often makes you appear weak and in order for you to achieve what you desire, you must at least give the impression of strength and confidence. I am not advocating rudeness, but be deliberate with your brain and mouth. Do not allow yourself to go on "nice guy" auto-pilot or get diarrhea of the mouth. Be different, abnormal, outrageous, extraordinary, and do not apologize to anyone for living the life YOU have chosen.

7.3 Tres Elements

As I have grown and matured along my journey, the elements that make up my ideal lifestyle have changed as well. Originally I was in survival mode and only focused upon meeting my own immediate needs. Gradually I had more than I needed at the moment, which afforded me the opportunity to take the time to search for meaning. After I made more than $100,000 when I was only 21-years-old and still was not happy, I wondered what more was out there. I had accomplished my early financial objectives, was free to do as I chose, and had the resources to do whatever I wanted.

But I remained unsettled, unsatisfied, and unfulfilled. This book is NOT just about how to get yourself in a position to make a lot of money. Money is just a tool. Alone, it will not make you happy. It just solves a lot of life's immediate challenges.

Life fulfillment became my lifestyle quest. I realized money alone was not enough because I had to have it all. I yearned to look in the mirror and FEEL on top of Everest – every day. It has often been said, shoot for the stars and at the very least, you will hit the moon. I believe that high expectations will reap high rewards. Because I had already achieved so much by such a young age, despite what others said, I felt invincible. My mental momentum was at an all-time high. But in order to live **fulfilled**, I had to come up with a clear definition of what that meant to ME. So I followed my prior pattern of asking other seemingly happy people what made them feel so good. Why were they so happy all the time? Then I shut up, listened, studied, and searched for their patterns. I employed exactly the same strategies which I have shared with you in this book. I sought to find the right people to add to my Life Fulfillment Teams. What I learned was amazing in its simplicity. Three key areas kept coming up. I heard three life themes over and over: Mental, Physical, and Spiritual.

7.3.1 Mental

I have already gone into this area with you thoroughly, so I will keep it short and to the point. When you control what goes into your mind, you control what comes out. You have the power to decide what is right for you and whether to implement the strategies within this book to make your ideal lifestyle a reality or not. Your past is only as strong as you allow it to be. When you commit to constant personal improvement, over time you will become unstoppable. Nobody can beat the person who will not allow themselves to be beaten. Life will eventually get tired of knocking you down and just give in to your demands.

Another common theme among the most successful and all around happiest folks I interviewed was helping other people. Karma is real and whatever you give in life does come back to you – good or bad. I believe life tests all of us constantly on this one. For example, a short time ago I was at my bank and in the process of doing a few transactions in the drive-thru, I ended up with $50 cash too much. I did not notice it until my next stop. I immediately drove back to the bank and gave the cash back. Who knows if it really mattered or not, but it mattered to me. Maybe the teller would have been reprimanded had I not returned the money. Maybe I would have received a speeding ticket for $200 on the way home. Who knows? I have had so many opportunities like this one to do the right thing. I do believe most people are inherently good, decent folks, and as a result, I meet many more good people. When I was younger and so angry about my childhood, I attracted other angry people.

Change your world outlook and your world changes.

This point brings me back to a moment when my life's purpose became crystal clear. In 1991, I had a great year and unfortunately, after earning so much money, I allowed it to go to my head. I became very showy, prideful, arrogant and unpleasant to be around, believing that my IQ indeed matched my income. I lost numerous key people who had been at the root of my success. I could not see this at the time and instead decided to point my finger at them as if they were the problem. But the truth has a funny way of catching up with people. Because I knew I was emotionally lost, I decided to shut my business down for a while and get a J.O.B. in an effort to regain a connection with where I began. In December 1991, I got a J.O.B. as a waiter in Tustin, California. One day about two weeks in, I was waiting on two ladies and they left me a $3 tip, which was appropriate for what they had ordered, but for some reason this tip in particular hit me hard. I remember picking up the money, going to the back of the restaurant, staring at these three $1 bills, and getting more and more angrier with myself. The thought that kept going through my head was, "My God, when I was running my business I could fart and make more than three dollars." I quit that J.O.B. immediately after this "personal moment" and never looked back again. This was a turning point and ever since that moment I have stayed grounded in my real life's purpose.

So in January 1992 I decided to dedicate my life to helping those who were willing to help themselves. I have spent a great deal of money, time, and effort creating tools so other people can learn to copy what I have found to work. I have had my share of run-ins with regulatory and governmental agencies. I have found that so many of the groups that claim to help others really are only motivated by manufacturing more problems, whether real or perceived, just to keep their funding rolling in. Most people just need someone to believe in them and a legitimate shot to make something of themselves. Providing the information and tools to those willing to do whatever it takes to enjoy their ideal lifestyle is what gives me zest and makes me FEEL fulfilled. Get your basic needs met as quickly as possible, which sales can certainly help you do, and then seek to find your own *purpose* in life – how you can help others. We all have our gifts. We all can be examples of what to do for other good people. I am thankful I have found my purpose.

7.3.2 Physical

Again, I believe a person's mental health is completely tied to their physical health. When I have been fat physically, I am almost always fat and lazy mentally at the same time. I believe life is rhythmic and it is perfectly fine to have ups and downs. This is not only to be expected and normal – I do not think I could exist happily in a state of *perfect* anything all the time. Zoltan used to say, "Food is fuel, Allen, just fuel." OK, but I really enjoy doughnuts, cheesecake, and prime rib. For me life is about savoring the good in moderation, which for an extremist like me is pretty darn tough sometimes. But I know how I feel when I am fat and I do not feel good. I beat myself up, get depressed, feel like everyone is looking at the *fat* guy, and play head games with myself. This is both sad and dangerous. I have seen other people who, rather than dealing with the health issue, end up driving away the good people in their lives by their unwillingness to do what needs to be done to become healthy once again.

In this book I have talked often about being fat, notice I do not call it overweight because I consider *overweight* to be too gentle a term for it. I am very familiar with what self-discipline plus diet and exercise can do for a person. I was once called *morbidly obese* and it stung because I was always the skinny kid growing up. The reason I focus upon *fat* for this point is that everyone understands obesity is a difficult challenge in our nation. It is connected to so many other life-threatening disorders such as diabetes and heart disease. But obesity, like any challenge, can be overcome with the right tools. The right mindset, coach, information, success routine, and support team will allow anyone to be in whatever physical shape they decide upon. Remember, I believe that enjoying your ideal lifestyle is absolutely tied to your level of productivity. So be honest, how much more productive are you when you feel and look good?

Take care of yourself. Who wants to be rich with poor health? I yearn to enjoy the fruits of my labor. I am unable to completely enjoy life when I get winded climbing a single set of stairs. Do whatever you need to do in order to feel and be healthy. All of the people on your Emotional Support Team will appreciate having you around for a long time. Finally, there is no question that when I feel better, I live better, and I have made a conscious decision to make becoming and remaining healthy a lifestyle habit. We all can be an example of what is possible when we employ the right tools. Physical actions will speed mental results.

7.3.3 Spiritual

A clean, light spirit makes the journey so much more enjoyable. I was raised Catholic and did everything that was required of me. However, as I have grown older, I no longer feel that organized religion is necessary for me. I have discussed this with many people and have come to a conclusion based upon what makes sense to me. Our world is a big place with lots of different kinds of people who have many different beliefs, but when you drill down to the essence of it, most of us believe there is a God, a creator. I do not believe I need to stand, kneel, sit, stand, kneel, sit, etc. once a week in order to have a relationship with God, which for me is what it means to be spiritual. The world does not revolve around any one of us, and in order for me to live well, I must remain as humble, appreciative, and open-minded as possible.

The happiest people I have found also seem to be the most welcoming and accepting of other people and their differences. My ideal lifestyle is to have the resources necessary to just live in peace with those around me, to be free to do as I choose with the resources I have, and to help whomever I choose when I choose. For me, church still remains a great place to belong so I can meet other good people in my community and reach out to those in need, but not a necessary ritual in order to feel whole. For me it is a private matter and I only go into this issue here because it is a very important third part of my Lifestyle Triangle. I have often said, "You can best judge a person by what they do when nobody is looking." For me, being spiritual, having a relationship with my higher power, helps me to keep my life vehicle between the lines and live up to the expectations I have laid down for myself.

You may have noticed I never used the word *balance* in regard to lifestyle. I cannot even tell you how many books I have read discussing this fallacy. I believe that to expect to achieve life balance is no different than going out to hunt the mythical unicorn. It does not really exist but sounds really meaningful to talk about. One week I may spend far more effort on my mental development than I spend praying, but the next week I may volunteer a great amount of time but not go to the gym at all. What I have seen in those who are at peace most of the time, those people who just seem to have a perpetual smile on their face, is the ability to recognize quickly when they are becoming too out-of-balance with any one area of their life and then work to correct it. Set yourself up to win at the game of life. Don't be too tough on yourself, keep it all in perspective. For all of us, life fulfillment is an amazing journey filled with self development, personal growth, building great relationships, overcoming enormous challenges, seeking to mature into the best each of us can be, and taking the time to have fun and enjoy the trip as much as possible. Instead of accomplishing any single objective along the way, life fulfillment for me is feeling mentally physically and spiritually healthy while on my lifestyle journey.

7.4　Truth # 7 Action Points

You are ready to begin traveling now, but still have some key decisions to make. Enjoying your lifestyle IS a way of life, not a destination. To be able to wake up each day and love your life is the most wonderful feeling of all. How can you ensure your journey is as enjoyable as possible?

A.　Choose your path. Everything starts with picking the right road to travel. You are now at a fork in the road and need to either choose Excuses or Performance. Whichever you choose will determine your typical way of life or mere existence. It is up to you, so begin your journey with eyes wide open. Understand and choose the right path for you. Which will it be?

B.　Stay between the lines. White lines are painted on both sides of the road for a reason; they provide you simple boundaries to keep your vehicle on the road, out of the ditch and moving forward. As you travel, keep the journey in its proper perspective. Stay out of your Comfort Zone as much as possible to keep sharp. Be willing to open your eyes to experience the wonderful joys life has in store for you. Be patient without getting lax. And never say *sorry* for allowing yourself to be who you really are, be willing to be YOU even when you are strange like me.

C.　Seek life fulfillment. Life balance is an unattainable myth that masochistic people strive to achieve, only to end up disappointed. Seek to live in a manner which makes you feel whole and at peace. Take nothing that does not belong to you and give more than you expect in return. Constant mental development, physical fitness, and spiritual enlightenment are the path I have chosen to live a fulfilled life. To rise every day enjoying the life you built and are blessed enough to live is what I want for everyone reading this book. The knowledge and power to do so is right within the palms of your hands and between your ears.

TRUTH # 8

Never ever quit!

I dedicate this truth to my dad, Joe Kronebusch, because he has been the single most significant example to me of a *never-say-die* and *never-give-up* mindset. I truly do not know how he did it. In 1979 he was a recently-divorced, single parent of two boys. First, he fought tooth and nail to get me out of the final foster home I had been put in. Then he fought to gain full legal custody of my little brother and myself. In Minnesota at that time, the father winning custody was a rarity to say the least. However, I do not think he had any clue what he was in for. Thankfully, when he adopted me in, he made a commitment to raise me no matter what, and I challenged him on that commitment every chance I could.

He gained nothing in the divorce but the house and us boys. He did what was right in the face of overpowering adversity without a safety net to catch him. In addition, shortly before the divorce, my parents lost their business. Then my dad's only financial vehicle was to break his back for the Chicago Northwestern Railroad in order to keep a roof over our heads. He did what had to be done without complaint. He is a great example of a real man.

8.1   Fear

On September 10, 1994, a beautiful fall day, I finally decided to stop talking about overcoming my fear of heights and actually did something about it. Climbing up on the silos to help my uncle Bernie took every bit of courage I could muster, but even then I was clipped to the ladder. Brian and I had talked about learning how to skydive for years and now we were finally taking action.

Mike, our instructor, or death coach as I nicknamed him, greeted us as we walked into the small building and sat down. The first thing Mike did was give us a contract to read and sign, which I read closely. I said to Mike, "It says here that even if you guys are at fault, my heirs cannot sue you. So if you packed me a lunch instead of a chute and I died, then too bad, so sad, nobody gets sued?" He said, "Yep" and then I signed up to become a skydiver. Fear has always really annoyed me. I spent much of my childhood afraid of one thing or another. Fear is one of the only kinds of friction that can slow your mental momentum. It can destroy your confidence when allowed to exist without being challenged. I was sick and tired of being afraid of heights. I felt like this fear had some kind of control over me, which I was allowing it to have, so I must face it head on in order to take the control back.

The entire day of skydiving training went like this – about 10 minutes was spent showing me how to pull the ripcord and the remaining five-plus hours was teaching us what to do if the chute did not open properly. I have to admit there were times when I questioned my sanity. The old question everybody asks was going through my head, "Why would you jump out of a perfectly good airplane?" However, I knew with absolute clarity WHY I was going to jump. Conquer a fear and I believe you gain a piece of your destiny. This was going to be one of those *moments* I would be able to talk about for the rest of my life. I would tell this same story to my grandchildren. Brian and I were taking the Path of Performance today and nothing was going to stop us.

Finally it was time to load into the plane and wouldn't you know it. - the heaviest guy had to jump first and guess who weighed the most? Three other jumpers all piled into this tiny little plane which resembled one of those clown cars at the circus. How could a pilot and FIVE other humans fit into something the size of a golf cart with wings? Finally Mike got in and then lucky little me. Mike closed the *door*, basically just a thin piece of transparent Plexiglas with a latch at the bottom. Then the engine began to whir and we started to move forward. Before you knew it, we were airborne and that is when the fun really began.

As we climbed higher, I watched my altimeter going up and Mike watched the color drain out of my face. He later said it almost looked like the two were linked. As I got whiter, I began to sweat. Not the "I'm running a marathon" sweat." This was the cold, clammy, sticky sweat a death row inmate must experience as they walk him to the electric chair. My first jump was a static line, which meant I was tied to the airplane, and when I jumped the plane would pull my ripcord for me. The plan was for me to jump somewhere around 3,300 feet. I knew this and as my altimeter reached 3,000 feet I was freaking out. Then it read 3,100, 3,200, and finally 3,300! Mike yelled, "DOOR OPEN!" And he flipped the latch. Whoosh! The door flung up and all I could hear three inches from my left ear was the wind. I peeked to my left and saw the Earth 3,300 feet below. God, it looked far away and all of a sudden this plane felt pretty damn comfortable. I didn't want to leave, but I had no option so I began to climb out.

The process is simple. Put both feet on a platform right above the wheel and your arms on the wing struts. Slide out and stand on the platform. Picture a guy scared witless 3,300 feet up in the air, strapped to an airplane with wind pounding him in the face and that was me. Then you have to slide your right arm to the right down the strut, then your left, step off the platform and HANG from the strut by just your hands. I looked back at Mike for his approval, hoping he wouldn't give me the thumbs up, but right then with a big Cheshire-cat grin, he gave me that damn overly-enthusiastic THUMBS UP! You are supposed to let go of the plane right then but ... wait just one second here.

If I let go, I am going to fall and there is no guarantee the chute will open. I said to myself, "OK, let go!" But I did not let go. Finally, after I remembered what Mike said on the ground, "Once you are outside of the plane, you will have to jump. We will not let you back in because it is too dangerous." I let go and the plane disappeared in the blink of an eye. I was falling fast but only for a few seconds and then I felt the opening shock and looked up to see a glorious parachute above me. I pulled my toggles to be able to steer, screamed at the top of my lungs, and felt the most intense rush I ever felt up to that point of my life. I did it! I overcame my fear. Courage is not the absence of fear. Courage is still doing what you are afraid of even when you are afraid of it. I felt courageous at that moment. This was one of those feelings nobody could ever take away from me.

Fear is the worst four-letter F-word in the English language. Fear creates analysis paralysis. Fear is at the root of anger, jealousy, hatred, self-doubt, and almost every other negative emotion a person can feel. Fear left unchallenged and unchecked is ugly because it is like a cancer that will grow and, if allowed, take over a person's mind and body. Fear will cripple your future by destroying all the good seeds you plant. I cannot stand fear and whenever I feel it, I get angry and face it. I have developed a personal pattern to overcome fear and like most of the really good information in life, the pattern is simple. I write down what I am afraid of, analyze it to see if it is rational or petty, then set out to do EXACTLY what I am afraid of in an effort to again prove to myself that fear has no control over me.

I did this same process with my fear of needles as I did heights. I bought a box of syringes and some saline and proceeded to self-inject every day for a month in order to finally get rid of this fear. Fear never completely goes away but it can be managed. My heart still quickens when I have to get a shot but I no longer get light-headed or faint. I am now much more able to just grin and bear it. I chose not to allow fear to keep me down or limit my life. This has led to some bizarre memories, such as when I was in the Florida Keys with my EO forum and jumped into the water with another crazy entrepreneur to battle with multiple hammerhead sharks. Maybe I took this one too far, but I am still alive and have a really cool story to tell.

Understand and accept you will encounter MANY fears along your journey. But what you do with that fear is what will determine whether you get to enjoy your ideal lifestyle or not. To run from fear is much like running from an angry dog, it WILL bite you over and over until either you hide or turn and face it. Even when you hide, the dog won't go away. Fear will just sit there next to the dog and wait until you get up enough courage to come out of your hiding spot. When you emerge, it will be right there to greet you again. So either face it now and move on, or face it tomorrow and the next day and so on.

Upon the plains of hesitation lie the bare bones of those who failed to go forward at the moment of victory. Whatever you fear most will happen because you will make it so. When you fear something, you will make it become a reality. When I feared that other people my own age would not accept me when I was in college, I hesitated to act. I hid and they did not even get the chance to meet me. Fear is a self-fulfilling prophecy – a vicious circle of negativity and despair. So either decide to control it by doing what you fear, or just sit back and accept its control over you and your future, and Regretsville's population will increase by one more. Fear is False Evidence Appearing Real. That's right – FALSE evidence that your mind tricks you into believing is real enough to hold you back. When you hesitate, victory is lost. Instead, be proactive by anticipating what might go wrong, and then do something so these things don't happen. Hire the best coach you can find to help you be better aware of the potholes coming up ahead in the road, and then you can proceed courageously avoiding them rather than fearing them.

My final point with fear is that YOU are in control of your own field. Don't allow other people's weed-seeds of fear to land in your field and take root. You have plenty of your own to deal with. Take control by facing whatever you fear head on. It is your life, so live it courageously. I have been crazy enough to jump a total of five times, three times from more than 12,000 feet where I pulled my own ripcord, and even went bungee jumping once. I was able to do this, create these amazing memories, all because of my ability to take away fear's power over me. I cannot be productive when I am afraid and neither can you. Fortune favors the bold!

8.2 Persistence

Nothing in the world can take the place of Persistence. Talent will not; nothing is more common than unsuccessful men with talent. Genius will not; unrewarded genius is almost a proverb. Education will not; the world is full of educated derelicts. Persistence and determination alone are omnipotent. The slogan 'Press On' has solved and always will solve the problems of the human race.

-Former President, Calvin Coolidge

Persistence is the quality of continuing on steadily despite the obstacles or challenges faced. When I started out selling safety equipment that November winter day in 1989, I did not have a car. I drove my motorcycle in the snow to my appointments because I had no choice. No matter which of the stories I have given you in this book, the common theme is persistence. The simple unwillingness to give up, no matter what, has been the cornerstone to my achievements. I am not the fastest runner but I won't quit. I am not the strongest person but I will not give up. I may not be the best at anything in life except persistence, and at the end of the day, I believe persistence is really all that matters.

The quote from President Coolidge has always moved me. Talent, genius, and education cannot surpass persistence. When someone won't give up, it is said that person has *heart*. And I believe it is very difficult, nearly impossible, to beat a person with heart because they just won't quit. Picture a sculptor staring at a gorgeous piece of raw, newly-quarried marble. He needs to break this stone into two pieces in order to make the sculpture he is envisioning. He hits it once, twice, thrice, and so on. He has struck 50 blows with his hammer and chisel but only made a small dent in this hunk of marble. Soon he has struck it 199 times, but still it remained in one piece. Sweating and tired, he contemplates giving up, but perseveres. On the 200th blow, the mighty stone breaks into two gigantic pieces right before his eyes. Was the 200th strike of his hammer somehow magical or different from number 199? No, of course not. Then what was it that broke the stone into two? It was the sum total of the entire 200 repeated strikes that finally overpowered the rock, forcing it to submit to the sculptor's will. This little story illustrates what I mean by persistence.

Life will constantly throw obstacles in your path, just as fear will be ever-present. What you do when confronted with these obstacles will determine your result. When you come to a wall, will you just stop and wait or will you attempt to go over, under, around, or finally through the wall? Nothing can stop you unless you allow it to. There is always a solution for the resourceful person who simply is unwilling to accept defeat. When you will not give up, life eventually will submit. It may not happen today, tomorrow, or even 199 days from now, but maybe on day 200 your dream will be realized. What happens if you stop at day 199? You never ever know how close you really are to victory; nobody does. Therefore quitting can never be an option. When you quit, it is sure to be right before life would have been willing to pay out the super jackpot, but somebody else more worthy than a quitter will end up getting the gold. The quitter just gets a lifetime of regrets to relive over and over again.

Sales is a numbers game. The best story I could ever tell you about sales and persistence happened to me in February 1990. I had gotten pretty good at the in-home safety-survey sales process I referenced before, so I wanted a new potentially more productive method to sell. I knew sales people were constantly approaching farmers by just walking onto the farm and striking up a conversation. I also knew by observation as a young boy that farmers often spend many thousands of dollars right on the spot. This got me to thinking and scary things happen when I think.

I gathered my fire extinguisher, order forms, calculator, and pen. Then I set out to sell. My goal was pretty simple. I would do 10 demonstrations each day no matter what. On Monday of the first week, I was excited and did my 10 but sold zero. Tuesday came and went and now with 20 presentations under my belt, I had absolutely nothing sold to show for it. Wednesday, Thursday, and Friday – still nothing. Week one down, 50 sales demonstrations later, and not a cotton-picking deal closed. I was questioning the intelligence of this decision but I kept going. I evaluated myself over the weekend, changed my pitch, and was ready to hit it again on the following Monday.

Week two comes and goes. I had been chased by dogs, snowed on, yelled at by a few less-than-friendly farmers and still NO sales. To say I was discouraged would have been the understatement of the decade. My girlfriend attempted to encourage me but I was feeling like a loser. No matter what I said, nobody wanted to buy from me and I began to take that personally, which was not very smart. However, life is sneaky because you never know when it is going to pay out.

Week three started like the last two. I had made more than 100 presentations with nothing to show for it except a lot of wasted gas. Two weeks wasted, or so I thought. On that first day of the third week, it all changed. I was doing the presentations to farmers near were my grandparents lived. I walked around the farm searching for the man of the house and when I said my name, he asked if I was related to Gerald and Theresa. When I told him they were my grandparents, he asked what I had to show him. This was a revelation because I was so angry and frustrated with most of my family and here was a time when I was pleasantly surprised. Because of building a reputation for hard work, integrity, honesty, and just being good, fun people, my grandparents on the Kronebusch side had inadvertently opened a door for me. I wasted no time stepping through.

This time I was able to really present and did so with a bit more confidence, which made all the difference. I made my first sale, a small one, but that is all that really mattered to me. With my renewed faith in myself and pride in my family name, I cleaned up that day and sold more than $1,000. That third week I sold more than $7,000 and my largest sale was only $500, which is really what finalized my belief that this business would work. To prove to myself this was not a fluke, I took my newly polished skill and confidence to an area that did not know my family name and proceeded to sell almost $5,000 in a later week, with still no single sale more than $500. I had played around with selling for three months, but now I was actually making it happen and closing some deals. What if I had quit at 50 presentations or even 100? Would you have kept going? The answer had better be YES because what choice do we really have if we are to enjoy our ideal lifestyle? We cannot take the Path of Excuses and give up when the going gets tough like sheeple do. We don't have the luxury of accepting defeat. We have to find a way to make it happen – no matter what. This single month in 1990 was an enormous personal growth moment for me and without it I would not live the life I do right now. I learned once again how not to take NO for an answer – there is ALWAYS a way to achieve what you decide upon. Sales is indeed a numbers game, the more presentations you do, the more you will learn, the better at communicating you will become, and the more deals you will close, as long as you don't quit before your growth occurs. I have always believed that sales is the average person's best shot to prove how above-average they really are.

Negativity must roll off of you like water off a duck's back. Be like an onion; when life beats up one layer of your being, shed it, and reveal a new one. To quit is the only real way to fail; everything else is just a temporary setback and ALL setbacks can be overcome. Why do I believe so strongly in this? Because God will not give us more than we can handle. And when the challenge appears to be overwhelming, instead of quitting, I believe somewhere somehow I must have the ability to succeed because otherwise I would not have been given this challenge.

8.3   Self-Discipline

Persistence and self-discipline are like two peas in a pod. You cannot have one without the other. In order to be persistent and keep up the good fight, you must be able to dig deep into your ability to go without, to live for the future and not simply for the moment. To be disciplined is to understand and live by delayed gratification. Do not allow yourself to remain a financially stupid work horse. There is more out there for you. Build your mind, then a business, and next use the business to buy all of the trinkets that make life fun. Otherwise, you will spend your precious time, emotional energy, and experience making someone else rich and remain their financial slave. You will make your choice with every purchase you make from now on. Every dollar is either a tool for consumption or lifestyle attainment – your choice. Successful people who remain successful and fulfilled learn to control their emotions and desires, not the other way around. Productive people decide what they are going to do and then go to work making their decision real. Successful people are the only ones who get to enjoy their ideal lifestyle; all others just exist to earn a living working for the successful.

8.4   Hope versus Want versus Need.

When you hope to achieve something you don't have a snowball's chance in heck of achieving anything. Do not confuse the word hope, as I mean it here, with the word faith. I specifically am referring to those people who go around and hope for this and that but do not ever seem to DO much of anything. Then there are the *wanters*. They want everything and because want is a little stronger than hope, they sometimes get it. However want is just not enough emotional energy for those of us who expect to enjoy our dream lifestyle. We NEED to do it.

Let me illustrate this point for you. If I were choking you with all of my strength and you were beginning to get lightheaded, I ask you, "What would you DO to get my hands off of your throat?" You NEED to breathe or you will die! There is no question that you would do whatever came to mind – kick me in the groin, gouge my eyes out, scratch, bite, whatever you could is what you would do because your life is on the line, true?

Now think of it like this, your LIFESTYLE is on the line. How you will live the rest of your life is on the line. I NEEDED to be free and there was nothing going to stand in my way. Because I NEEDED it, I stuck with it. I held on for dear life and eventually I was stronger than whatever garbage life threw in my path. Finally, because I NEEDED to succeed so badly, life eventually gave in and as a result I have been able to enjoy my idyllic lifestyle instead of just surviving by earning a living renting my time to the highest bidder.

8.5   Truth # 8 Action Points

As you move forward, life will constantly test you. Are you up for the challenge? Or will you just give up and settle for buying a small place in Regretsville using someone else's money? You have the power to control your outcome in the game of life. Fear, pain, and challenges are a part of life, and they will never completely go away, so what are you going to DO to ensure you are always going forward no matter what?

A.   <u>Overcome fear</u>. Whatever you fear most, you should do. Take control of what scares you. Conquer a fear and gain a piece of your destiny. Fear is just false evidence that your mental weeds are attempting to use to scare you into staying stationary. Rip them out by the roots and throw them away. You decide what your life will be and you decide not to allow your fear to be the friction slowing the mental momentum you fought so hard to build.

B.   <u>Remain persistent</u>. Winning is the unwillingness to give up. Continue to strike the marble until IT gives up because you never will – this is how you win. Life puts up a good front and attempts to act tough, but life always concedes to the person who refuses to give in. This is the way it has always worked. The victor is not necessarily the smartest, fastest, or richest, but always is the person with the most *heart*.

C.   <u>Develop your self-discipline.</u> Learn about the game of money. Study how people get rich and with this information, position yourself for success. It is very tough to succeed when you spend most of your time helping other people get rich by trading your personal productivity for useless depreciating trinkets. There is nothing wrong with being a workhorse, but be sure you are pulling your own wagon, not someone else's, by giving in to the temptation of immediate gratification. Ownership and directing of your personal productivity, while remaining emotionally disciplined, are paramount.

TRUTH # 9

Learning to fish will set you free!

There are a lot of good people out there who work hard every day to make this country what it is. For many of these people, owning their own business some day is a critical part of their American Dream – to be able to be somebody and stand tall as an independent person. Many have attempted to leap from a J.O.B. to business ownership and failed. The battlefield of business is literally littered with their dead and dying bodies just ripe for the vultures to pick their bones clean. Why do so few succeed?

For almost 20 years I have been building people and businesses, so I did not just wake up one morning with an epiphany and come to this conclusion. After being in and out of the trenches of battle, along with constant observation (People Studies), I have seen and experienced this one fact repeatedly. I have found that the reason 90 percent of all small businesses fail is because not enough people know how to sell and practice the skills of selling. Sales is negotiating, conflict resolution, mediation, seeing opportunities, developing a must-do-attitude, being resourceful, performing, effectively communicating, growing personally, and so much more.

Once you have made the decision to take ownership of your own productivity rather than continue renting it to help someone else become rich, you must then develop your sales skills. Sales is the fall-back or safety net of the business owner. Parents often recommend to their children, "No matter what you want to do in your life be sure to get your college degree because you will always have it to fall back on." When you can sell, you can ALWAYS generate more money and as long as you have money, your business can stay in business. Every day you are in business for yourself you will learn something new and grow. Unlike when you have a J.O.B., when you own a business your experience is not the typical pattern of one year repeated over and over. When you are the owner and have 20 years of experience, you really have *twenty* full years of new and different challenges, which you overcame in order to stay in business. These are years of real experience to draw upon for the rest of your life, which nobody can take away. Don't fool yourself. At a J.O.B., your position can be taken away for any reason at any time, no matter how much experience you might have. This is why I believe sales is life's safety net because when you can sell, you are in control of your productivity and will never go hungry! If you still want to work a J.O.B., think about this: companies are *always* looking for new people who can sell but may not be looking to fill other skilled positions. A company can never have enough money-generating machines. When you can make the dollars flow because of your skill, somebody will always want you on their team.

Sales is the ability to transfer belief from one person to another using effective communication. Belief is really the same as faith and they both are just intense emotional feelings about something. It could be religion, politics, a product or service, a company, another person – anything. Communication is just taking how you feel and putting it into words. But sales is *effective* communication and to communicate effectively requires training, discipline, self-study, and a lot of practice. I have seen countless people claim they do not know how to sell, cannot sell, have never done sales, are not the sales-type, and simply are scared to do it. Some people act as if sales is this mysterious thing that is so hard to grasp or understand. Baloney! This is of course how I feel now after years of experience, but I still remember the butterflies in the stomach, sweaty palms, and dry mouth when I started. I was out of my comfort zone when I began selling but sure am glad I did not allow my fear and nervousness to stop me from living my dream.

9.1 Sales philosophy according to me (a.k.a. "The Rant")

An old adage says, "Give a man a fish and you feed him for a day. Teach him how to fish and he will feed himself for a lifetime." This is the entire premise upon which this book and my coaching style have been developed. I wrote this to help those of you willing to help yourselves and only coach those actually willing to do what it takes to improve. My purpose is to give you truths and functional tools and explain them clearly so you will immediately apply them to better your life. I have often heard it said that knowledge is power, but I must add to that statement. Only APPLIED knowledge is powerful. To learn is fine, but to apply what you learn is what really matters. As I stated, my desire is to provide you accurate information, but without a sense of urgency you may not apply it. You create a sense of urgency by having a reason to do something and a deadline to do it by. I did some research to prove why you need to take ownership of your personal productivity NOW before it is too late for you.

Here are statistics that show the reality of the **average** American citizen's existence gathered from the U.S. Census Bureau and the U.S. Department of Labor's Bureau of Labor Statistics.

1. An average individual earns annually only $26,036 before taxes.

2. An average household of 2 ½ people earns a measly $48,201 annually before taxes, AND they have a debt load of $18,700, which represents their credit cards and other consumer loans, excluding mortgages.

3. The average cost of purchasing a home is $291,000.

4. An average annual household's cost of living is $37,327, which only includes the items listed below. Notice there is no education, entertainment, tobacco, 401K contributions, or alcoholic beverages included.

    - Food = $5,931.
    - Home maintenance = $6,362.
    - Transportation = $4,800.
    - Healthcare = $2,664.
    - Mortgage payment (housing) = $15,684.
    - Clothing = $1,886.

I am an eternal optimist. I seek to find a positive spin on every situation, which makes it much easier to identify opportunities and seize them. But here with these facts, even I am struggling to see the positive. I don't even understand how the average family of 2 ½ people pays everything the government says they do in these statistics because the math does not seem to work out. How can you make $48,201, then pay taxes, and still have enough to support a basic-existence living which costs $37,327? I guess this is why people's debt load seems to be increasing each year. **When** you spend more than you make, I guess you need to use other people's money (debt) to cover the gap in order to survive.

Honestly evaluate this picture, what do you see? Forget the statistics for a moment – what do you see with your own eyes, in your own family? Do you see people seeming to work harder and harder just to keep up? Why is it that not too long ago my grandfather could specialize by ONLY farming, but my family members currently farming must work an additional J.O.B. or two to make ends meet?

The way of thinking used in the Industrial Age is dead and gone. The ability to get a J.O.B., then be a loyal company-man and work hard for 20 or 30 years and retire with a company pension is fast becoming a distant memory. I am so thankful I saw the writing on the wall when I was young and therefore chose to take a different path, or else I would be in the same position busting my tush wondering why I cannot seem to get ahead. We are now in the Information Age. You can be the ostrich with its head in the sand like most sheeple and attempt to ignore this reality to your own peril.

Our leaders have long pushed off the problems of one generation onto another, but eventually the bill will come due. Soon, very soon, we are anticipated to have more people drawing from Social Security than paying into it – how is that going to work? AARP is certainly not going to allow the government to default on paying the obligations promised to our senior citizens, but where will the money come from?

I have discussed this information with literally hundreds of people in the past few years. Some understand and some just don't want to see the truth. Answer this one, "Who writes the tax laws? God?" No, of course not, even though it appears some people have God-complexes when they behave as if the government owns our productivity simply because we are allowed to live in

America. Who writes the tax codes, rich or poor people? I don't believe many bureaucrats ask the bum on the street corner for his opinion. There is a saying, "He who has the gold makes the rules and he who makes the rules KEEPS the gold." This is not rocket science but it irritates me like nothing else. Rich people write tax rules to service other rich people and I accepted years ago that I was never going to be able to change this by myself alone. Instead, I first chose to study the rules in order to learn how to use them to enjoy the lifestyle of my dreams and second bring this insight to many struggling people in our country. People who own their own productivity are making it big and living the lifestyles they desire. Just because you have not yet succeeded, doesn't mean you won't in the future – your past does not determine your future.

I also ask people during my rants, "When you work for someone else as an employee, why is the government ALLOWED to take its cut first?" I have not been an employee since I was 19 years old for good reason. Fortunately I became sick and tired of being ripped off while I was very young and sought out the path of the rich in order to end up living like the rich. I am no different than you; other than I was willing to do whatever it took to benefit from my OWN productivity (a limited resource). An employee may pay the government first, but does a business owner? Absolutely not. The government graciously allows me as a business owner to pay all of my legally allowable tax deductions FIRST. If there is anything leftover, then I pay the government its cut of the spoils. Why does the government allow me to do this? Is it because they are so caring and nice and think I am a swell guy? Of course not.

This is my take on it – I think the government gives certain allowable advantages to business owners because we employ all of the ostriches and sheeple, from whom the government gets its necessary income stream to keep its outdated bloated machinery working. Right or wrong, as a business owner, I have sometimes felt like a financial slave trader. Dangle the dependent mind-numbing carrots of J.O.B. security, fancy title, guaranteed level of income, 401K, pension, paid vacation, expense account, etc. in front of a person who has been conditioned since birth to get and keep a good J.O.B. and *POOF* they quickly trade their own productivity for these trinkets and beads often because they do not know any better or are too afraid to do anything else. Business owners get to live the good life, while employees struggle to scrape out a living. Once again, I am not sympathetic to the person who, once they are made aware of this, still chooses to work a J.O.B. No, their own struggle then becomes their own fault. Remember the difference between ignorance and stupidity is the lack of being exposed to accurate information. If after learning the truth the person still chooses to live in Regretsville, I will accept it because I don't have to live their life. I learned NONE of what I now know to be truth, of how the real world works, from my trusted teachers in school. Unfortunately they just taught me how to be a good sheep, find the best paying J.O.B. I could, pay my taxes, and struggle to eek out a life on the scraps left over. How many even know the real reason behind The Boston Tea Party?

I did not make the rules of the game of money. However, I took the time necessary to study the rules with an open mind while constantly searching for the truth by talking to rich and/or successful people. Gradually I learned how the GAME is really played. I will have an employee when it is absolutely necessary and required by law, but I have spent a great deal of time and money studying the existing independent contractor versus employee rules / laws. As a result, I seek to teach others how to live free by taking ownership of their own productivity. By understanding the rules of the game, anyone can live free rather than be subservient to the man.

The government does not create revenue – it only takes and redistributes. Who has the government established such a wonderfully successful pattern of taking from, almost to the point of sucking them dry? The middle class – the backbone of our nation. In so many ways, the middle class is what keeps our nation strong and the current financial leader of the world instead of just another economic disappointment. The rich did not build this nation alone. They employed the middle class and for a very long time that relationship worked out well, but is it still working? If it ain't broke, then I say don't fix it, leave it alone. But when an average family has to have both the husband and wife work one or two J.O.B.s in order to live the so-called American Dream, I believe something is broken. I am but one person and all I can do is tell you the truth as I see it – until you own your own productivity, you will continue to be broke. How you break free from the Cycle of Struggle, the "rat race", is up to you. I believe developing your sales skills is something that will solve all of our problems. America was founded by and built by sales people. Our founding fathers did not have 100 percent support from the other colonists before rebelling against mother England. No, they SOLD their fellow Americans on the idea of "live-free-or-die-trying", which had to be one fantastic sales pitch. Think about it, everyone who went against the English Crown and lost was not only to be killed, but their possessions seized and families disgraced. WOW! Yet these people still rose up and did what they believed needed to be done. After all, sales is just the transfer of one person's belief to another, but the ability to effectively transfer belief is very powerful indeed.

I believe the average American family must take control of their own productivity. By doing so, we will remain competitive at the world level and the American Dream will stay alive for our children to inherit. It is our duty to learn to sell because this skill is a crossover skill. It is not only useful in the office, but in the home, place of worship, school, and every other corner of our society. How many of our current prison inmates would not have chosen to break the law if only they had believed they could do better and had a skill to use to make that belief real? However,

I am a realist and not terribly sympathetic to people who choose to do stupid things. I am simply emphasizing we had better get ourselves onto the right track once again. China is not going to get any less industrial and they have four times our population. Look at India and all of the other Asian countries who want a piece of this ever developing global economy. America will soon become like some European countries – outdated with an entitlement mentality. My father drove into my brain that nobody owes any of us anything – we all must get what we desire on our own. I believe in helping all who are willing to produce in our country, no matter how young or old, to learn how to sell so we can right our nation's ship. There won't be as many herds of ostrich and sheeple to keep penned up on the Path of Excuses. More people will open their eyes, get awfully tired of witnessing what I have, and as a collective group of leaders make significant positive changes occur (***The $100,000,000 March*™**). However, I am but one obnoxiously loud passionate voice searching for others.

In the Information Age, as I see it, your ability to SELL your ideas is as important as being able to breathe. Applied sales skills = success. It does not matter if you are selling light-boxes online to help people overcome the winter blues or creating the ability for people to share their video clips. The skills taught in this book about life and sales will make all the difference between success and failure for those who apply them: *effective communication of your beliefs, creating win–win situations, persistence, overcoming your own past and current fears, developing teams of people to drive your vision, and so much more.*

When you are able to sell, you no longer need an employer to give you a fish. Therefore the employer and the government are no longer allowed to control your productivity. Learning to sell is exactly the same as learning to fish with a single fishing pole. Practice constantly – learn which bait to use, how to create interest by the fish, set the hook, and reel them in without breaking your line. Do this well and you will never be hungry again. Learn to fish with a pole and you have just gained ownership of your own time, emotional energy, and experience. Now you control exactly where your limited assets are directed. Instead of making your boss prosperous, now you are making yourself successful by providing value to your fellow man. You are in the driver's seat controlling your own vehicle.

9.2   Freedom is NOT free

This all sounds good, but you must produce in order to live free. When you are in control, security only comes from your own performance. Your ability to catch that fish will determine whether you and your family will eat or go hungry. As your skills improve, so does your productivity level. And your skills WILL improve because sales is just a numbers game. The more people you talk to, the better at communicating and producing you will become. As your productivity improves, so does your ability to no longer just provide for yourself, but now for your spouse and eventually your children. When you can sell, you become a warrior who goes out into the world and slays the dragon in order to bring it home and feed the family. For all of time and in every culture, warriors are respected and honored because they PRODUCE. To continue numbly taking the fish from your employer, renting your time, trading your hours for dollars, only continues to give that employer and the government power to control and direct your productivity. We have come full circle from when I started this book because here again I stress, it is your choice. Again I stress to you, "DECIDE on what kind of lifestyle you NEED."

Only 5.63 percent of all Americans currently earn more than $100,000 per year (US Census Bureau 2006) and just 1.4 percent of all Americans, only 14 out of every 1,000 people, will ever become a millionaire. Just because this is not happening to you does not mean it is not happening all around you. The difference between successful people and those who just continue living in the normal day-to-day grind existing paycheck to paycheck is how they think – how their mental muscle processes information. Remember, both the millionaire and bum on the street have the same 24 hours each day to work with but their lives are completely different. I do not get discouraged by statistics because they are just numbers. Instead I choose to study statistics in order to figure a way to use them to motivate myself on my journey to my ideal lifestyle. This data excites me because knowing the truth about what is wrong is at least half of what is needed in order to overcome the challenge. Also, it proves that earning $100,000 and becoming a millionaire *is* possible. If other people can do it, I believe I can too. I just need to figure out what they are doing differently and then change my own thinking, actions, and habits to match theirs. From my research, I was able to confirm every 126 minutes in 2005 and 2006, a person somewhere in America became a new millionaire. That means within a little more than every two-hour time period, while most people were eating dinner, watching a couple TV shows, or renting their time to their employer, there was a real person who, because of choosing a different path, was able to live the lifestyle of their dreams. While you slept, four new millionaires were created. While you commuted today to work and home again, a new person broke free from the chains of financial destitution. Why them and why not YOU?

I researched even further and found even more information on these same self-made millionaires. I learned these successful people credited one specific skill as one of the top three factors that most led to them becoming a millionaire. I'm sure you guessed it by now, the ability to sell! After all, sales is just effective communication. Sales is the ability to get another person to believe as you do about a product or idea, and therefore be willing to buy it. I sell ideas to my wife, my children, and the people I do business with. I even sell them to myself. I am selling all the time, which just means I am communicating in a <u>deliberate</u> manner to create <u>win-win</u> situations which <u>help my customers get what they want</u>. As a result, the people I surround myself with and I get to enjoy the lifestyle we desire. I sell myself to other people and sell myself on WHY to keep persevering no matter which obstacles life throws in my way. The ability to get others to believe in you and your ideas is critical to making the journey to life-fulfillment.

9.3 The noodle-puller teaches how to fish

Telling is not selling. I strive to not tell my wife what we are going to do or my sons how they must act. Rather, I choose to use effective communication techniques that empower them to make decisions for themselves. They usually choose what I wanted them to, but not always, which often creates a learning opportunity for me. Because of not seeking to control others, I am rewarded with new and different ways of looking at the same issues. Sales is give and take – the process of developing win-win situations so all parties walk away *feeling* as good as possible. When you work in a J.O.B., typically you work for a boss and bosses usually tell and do not sell. I will illustrate this point to you.

Let us say you have a wet spaghetti noodle lying on one side of a kitchen table. Your goal is to get it to the other side. What does a leader do? What does a boss do? A boss will push it and the noodle, like the employee, gets smushed. Over time, the employee gets knocked down so many times, he loses heart and gives up. He is trapped in Regretsville between his obligations (family, mortgage, car payment, etc.) and his employer, and the employer knows it. The employee feels stuck even though he oftentimes won't admit it. No, it's better to just keep on keeping on, rather than make waves. After all, he wouldn't want to lose his J.O.B., because what would he do then? But he does have other options like I have often stated in this book – he just has to be willing to recognize and seize them.

The leader on the other hand gets in front of each person on the team, grabs their hand and LEADS BY EXAMPLE. Much like your coach led when tied to you while climbing Everest on the Path of Performance, the leader pulls the noodle across the table. Leaders help to elevate you, not keep you down, so eventually you build your confidence enough to be able to get yourself up off of your knees, stand on your own two feet, and take control of your own life. A leader teaches you HOW to fish and helps you set yourself free. What is a leader? A leader is just a person who SELLS their IDEAS in order to help lead their team members to victory. A leader really only wins when their team members win, because their success is totally connected to that of their followers. Because of this win-win relationship, the team members follow the leader wherever they may go with eyes wide open, by choice, instead of as a result of desperation or necessity. The team trusts that their leader has their best interests at heart and they are correct.

9.4   Leaders fish with a net

Instead of selling a product like a sales person, the leader inspires and motivates other people to take actions that help the team prosper. The leader accomplishes this by selling ideas to their troops. A general in the Army must sell the soldiers on why to go to battle, which could possibly mean giving up their own lives. The soldier is scared but goes anyway. Why? From the great General George S. Patton, old Blood and Guts himself, one of the greatest military leaders of ALL time, I pulled these quotes for you.

"Lead me, follow me, or get out of my way."

"May God have mercy upon my enemies, because I won't."
"Attack rapidly, ruthlessly, viciously, without rest, however tired and hungry you may be, the enemy will be more tired, more hungry. Keep punching."

"In war the only sure defense is offense, and the efficiency of the offense depends on the warlike souls of those conducting it."

"America loves a winner, and will not tolerate a loser, this is why America has never, and will never, lose a war."

He led during our country's greatest war in which our very way of life was threatened, and because of leaders like him, we still speak English instead of German, and we remain FREE to build our ideal lifestyles. General Patton and all great leaders SELL their ideas to inspire and motivate their team. First, learn how to sell a *product*, which is much easier than selling an *idea*. You can see, touch, smell, taste, and experience a product, but an idea is intangible. An idea only exists in the mind of the leader until the leader's belief in their idea is **sold** (effectively communicated) to the team. When the sale is made, the team will take ownership of the idea for themselves and as a result take action to make the idea real.

The ability to sell your ideas is where the really big money is, but like a baby learning to walk, you too must first learn to crawl. Develop your abilities to effectively communicate and build relationships by selling a product. When you are ready, then graduate to selling your ideas to others and lead them to better lives. Leaders serve those whom they lead. Leaders help people by inspiring them to believe they CAN be more and then lead them along the path to get there.

You have the choice in financial vehicles – which will you drive? You can either earn 100 percent of a single set of hands or 1 percent of 100 sets of hands. Being able to lead effectively is just like fishing with a net. No longer are you limited to a single fishing pole because you are leading a team consisting of others fishing with poles and the productivity level is the same as if you were using a net. Your haul of fish will be much greater, which will provide a surplus of life's abundance for you to share with those you care about. Massive amounts of emotional energy and money will fill your life as a result of helping other people get what they desire. I once heard someone say, "Care more for the wallet of the person you lead than you do about your own. As a result, yours will never be empty." So let me teach you the basics about how to sell. Use these no matter what situation you might be in. You could be attempting to get a date or be elected to office – the specific situation matters not. Both instances require effective communication and eventual relationship-building in order to be successful.

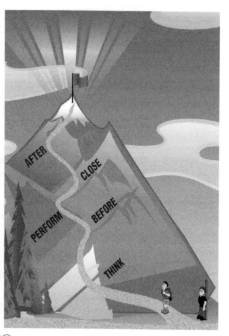

9.5   "Here   fishy, fishy, fishy ..."

The Sales Process. I created this image of <u>Victory Mountain</u> to illustrate the process of making a sale. Obviously this mountain is the Path of Performance and your coach is right next to you to help along the way. You have your pack properly prepared and now you are ready to climb to your success. Every time you make a sale, you have crested this mountain and life allows you to plant your flag so the whole world can see you are a warrior. Reach the peak enough times and your confidence in the process grows exponentially, eventually to become limitless. This same process works effectively to close the deal for any sales opportunity life provides. The process of making a sale is: first create and/or discover a valid NEED within your customer for what you are selling, then fill that NEED by closing the deal, which is all accomplished by the use of effective communication.

9.5.1 Think

Prepare your mind to create the NEED. No matter what you are selling or which sales method you choose to use, the basic skeletal structure of the sales process is the same. You should employ all five key elements to ensure success. First you must think like a successful person in order to mentally be in the right place to see and seize opportunities as they present themselves. Most of this book has been focused on the subject of mindset because it is the most important element of all. I can attempt to teach a blind and deaf monkey the basics of sales and it may still close a deal or two. However without the proper mind for the seeds to take root in, the poor monkey will never become a sales pro. Mindset is not something you develop once and are done. I see and experience new ways to look at and understand the world every day. By remaining open-minded, willing to see the truth and seeking to understand what is new and different, it keeps me sharp so I may continue to enjoy my ideal lifestyle. As you grow in the other four areas (Before, Perform, Close, After) – *never* stop developing your mind.

9.5.2 Before

Proper preparation is critical to success at anything you do and sales is no different. Prepare for the win, especially when it comes to taking ownership of your productivity. Here are some valuable questions to ask yourself and decisions you must make before you sell anything to anyone.

1. <u>How will I sell?</u> Decide which method of selling you will begin your product-sales career in: retail, multi-level, direct sales, telemarketing, or on the Internet. Each has advantages and disadvantages. Whichever you choose is fine, just pick one.

2. <u>To whom will I sell?</u> Will you be selling to private individuals as Business to Customer (B to C), or Business to Business (B to B), or finally Business to Government, (B to G). Seek out what interests you. These are three different animals. Selling to a private person is often times quite different than to a business, and the government is a whole new challenge to deal with. Whatever most appeals to you must be at the root of your choice, not whichever will provide the greatest income opportunity. Remember, money comes as a result of actions you take, not the reason to take that action in the first place.

3. <u>What will I sell?</u> Will it be a product, service, or simply information? Each has its own share of challenges and benefits. Find something that gets you excited. I have always believed that an excited person will find a way to produce. Sales is 90 percent WHY (emotion) to sell but only 10 percent HOW (logic) to sell. Sales training is important, but selling something you like and believe in is more important. When you believe in what you are selling, it is easy for you to transfer that belief (*effectively communicate*) to another person.

4. <u>When will I start?</u> Obviously you know my position on this one. To continue to trade your productivity any longer for shiny beads and trinkets, after you have read

this book, would be a crime. Even a sales J.O.B. that paid a salary plus commission would be an OK start. Maybe you want to be like the frog in the pot and transition more slowly. That is up to you and perfectly fine as long as you are making progress toward YOUR ideal lifestyle. For me, the pursuit of enjoying your lifestyle is much like being pregnant – either you are or you are not – period. Either you own your productivity or you don't. At the end of the day, do what is right for you!

5. <u>Where will I start?</u>   What team will you join?   I experienced much of my sales development in the position of being the owner. If I was to do it all over again, I would have done it slightly differently. Rather than so quickly seeking to start and build my own completely independent company, I would instead seek out and join an existing successful business which would teach me how to succeed. Learning by both participation and observation is very helpful.

By joining an existing team, I believe I would have been even more productive than I was at an even younger age. The group would have provided me a built-in Emotional Support Team, Peak Performance Team, and even some members of a Task-Doer Team right from the start. The team would have been highly motivated to teach me what they did right and the mistakes they made as well. Why? Because they would have profited from my success as well. This would have been a win-win situation – I learn and grow and we all make lots of money.

After I had grown enough in product sales, I could work to develop into a successful leader of other sales people. I don't regret the path I took because it worked out well for me at the time. I am who I am now because of the severe ups and downs of that path. My childhood made me a survivor, which became necessary to endure the tough times of my journey. I have written this book so YOU will have the greatest likelihood of success! Even though I believe everyone should develop sales, management, and leadership skills, it does not mean they have to copy every element of what I did verbatim in order to succeed.

Maslow's *Hierarchy of Needs* makes the point that once you successfully meet your basic human needs (food, clothing and shelter), you will then want to be part of a team that makes you feel proud of that team. In addition, you will also seek to gain a sense of personal accomplishment, to feel like you are somebody special. Find and/or build the right team and all of your emotional and intellectual needs can be met in an environment that will nurture and encourage your continual growth.

6. <u>How do I find the right team?</u> This book's purposes are to open your eyes to the truth, help to create that energy to choose the right vehicle, and give you the tools you need in order to develop your thinking so you can enjoy the lifestyle of your dreams. Again, the single most important thing is to get STARTED! No matter what you decide to do, take action now!

A word of caution to the wise: No matter which team you join, understand you are not married to that opportunity. The moment someone is dishonest with you or promises something to you or your customer and does not fulfill it or have someone above them in the organization fulfill it, consider finding a new team. **Hire slowly and fire fast.** This is your lifestyle pursuit and you have no time to waste with poor-quality people. You will have to use your common sense because no person or organization is perfect, but you will have to be the judge as to the *intentions* behind any mistake. Trust your gut feeling because it is usually right. If the mistake was an honest, forgivable one, then move forward cautiously with the team. But if the intention was to mislead or be deceptive in any way, leave quickly and never look back. Sales is a wonderful field with great people and companies, but like any industry we also have people who learn this powerful skill and use it for ill gain.

Achieving your ideal lifestyle is highly dependent upon your level of productivity. Now that you own it, you should demand that what you own is actually worth something, wouldn't you agree? Therefore do not allow yourself to waste time while on an unproductive team. When you look back over your time with your team and can honestly say you have given 110 percent but are still not experiencing a high level of continual growth, then it is time to sit down with your coach and voice your dissatisfaction. If nothing is done to fix the situation, leave and seek out a new team, because you may have outgrown this group. I have outgrown many friends and coaches. When I outgrow them and no longer believe they can help me move forward, it is time for me to be strong enough to move on. We do not have any time to waste – life only pays on results!

7. <u>What will I do with all the money?</u> Assume the win. Prepare now. Be proactive. Begin to develop relationships with key future Peak Performance Team members. These people will help you intelligently place the money you generate. The money will flow very well when you apply everything taught to you in this book – so prepare now. Don't be like the classic sales idiot who spends all their money on shiny beads and trinkets and when they have an off week or month, fall immediately into financial ruin.

Just because you are involved in sales does not mean you know how to handle money. Specialize in doing what you do well and hire others to assist you in those areas that will solidify your financial future. DEDFIL yourself constantly. By Developing your Emotional Discipline, Financial Intelligence, and Leadership skills, you will earn and keep a lot of money. It matters less how much you make than how much you keep out of what you make. The financial winner prepares for the windfall NOW (before), so when it happens, and it will, they are prepared to seize the opportunity. Then all the other people around the winner can think how lucky the winner is, but the winner knows the truth. It was not luck; it was preparation that ensured the prosperity.

Earning $100,000 a year is all right but it does not buy what it used to. By DEDFIL-ing yourself, you will be on the right track to a lifestyle filled with choices. Maybe $100,000 will be enough for you, but after taxes there is not as much left as one might think. Buy a decent house in a nice neighborhood, drive two cars, have a boat, and just a few of the other luxuries that make life fun and $100,000 is not enough. But you could earn $250,000 or more as a sales leader. It is all in your future when you apply what is in this book, so prepare for it NOW! Lasting positive lifestyle change does not happen overnight. To break from the herd will take time, so be willing to pay your dues experiencing both defeat and victory, until you are strong enough to lead.

After you have answered these questions and you are ready to start selling, then prepare for the actual sales presentation. Here are some of the most important items to prepare in advance before ever talking to a customer.

1.   <u>Wants.</u> Ask your fellow team members a lot of questions to understand what the customer will really want, before ever approaching the customer. When you are aware of what they will want, next be sure you can deliver.

2.   <u>Reputation.</u> Do your due diligence to ensure your company will honor all of the commitments you will make to your customer in order to close the sale. Your reputation is on the line.

3.   <u>Research.</u> Know your product better than anyone else. It is also very important to know your competitor's product as well as you know your own.

4.   <u>Incentives.</u> Learn exactly what incentives you can offer to the customer to effectively create a sense of urgency, which will get the customer to take action and close the sale as quickly as possible.

5.   <u>Practice.</u> Practice your presentation until all of those people around you on your Emotional Support Team could do it as well as you because they have heard it so often. Do it in front of a mirror to watch your facial expressions and body language. Whenever possible, practice in front of another person and ask for constructive comments, or videotape yourself and watch it, looking for areas to improve. You need to study your mannerisms even if you sell over the phone because everything comes through that receiver. Practice does not make perfect, perfect practice makes perfect, so close your eyes and repeatedly visualize the *perfect* presentation from start to finish. Do this often enough and what you see in your mind will become reality.

6.   <u>How to dress.</u> Be deliberate in how you dress. Even if you are selling over the phone, dressing and behaving

in a certain way while you are on the phone will project professionalism. How you dress is even more critical when you are face-to-face. Dress like your customers, because your goal should be to get them to like you. People we like are typically people just *like* us. People usually choose to do business with others they like, and I have found that how you dress has a big impact upon how quickly someone likes you, or if they ever like you. When I sold to farmers, I dressed as farmers do and when I sold to businesses I dressed as they did. The point is to mimic your audience.

9.5.3 Perform

Life pays only those who perform! Take all your preparation work and put it into action. Pretend you are on stage *performing* for the audience. Step up, deliver your lines, and make the crowd go wild. Performing is all about creating the NEED!

When people NEED to do something, they will act. When they only hope or want to do something, action may or may not occur. You must understand what must be done in your industry in order to build a Sense of Urgency (Reasons and Deadlines), thereby creating a NEED so your customers will act. This is the most important thing your sales coach and fellow team members can teach you – how to inspire the action you want on the part of your customer. Action is not accidental and your customer will typically not act how you want them to without you creating the NEED and developing an urgent reason to act by your deadline. Did you ever wonder why there is a sale, or even worse, a Going-out-of-Business sale seemingly every other day all around town? Reason + Deadline = Sense of Urgency to Act and the desired action is to have the customer buy.

The bigger the NEED created, the larger the sale you will close.

The better you perform, the more your customer will tend to like you. Even if you are selling gold bars and I don't like you, then I probably don't trust you either. When I don't trust you, I will be suspicious that your product may not be gold bars after all. Maybe you just took some cheap lead bars and had them gold-plated to fool me.

This is why I strive to mimic my customer as much as possible. My goal is to have them feel that I am just like them. I will seek to duplicate how they dress, breathe, sit, talk, and act. When I was face-to-face and they offered me a beer when I was only 19, I took the beer. When they asked me to join them for dinner, I joined and found many positive things to compliment the chef on – all compliments were always genuine. I believe you should always be genuine and not just another BS artist. When I sold to farmers, I did not wear a tie because they didn't either. When I sold ideas to other business owners or bankers, I did not wear jeans unless the circumstances called for casual dress. My point is that I am totally focused upon my customer. I am engaged 100 percent in creating their NEED in what I am selling in order to benefit them by filling the need later in my performance.

I feel I must point out that I will not allow myself to become a sales whore *(an offensive term for somebody who is regarded as willing to set aside principles or personal integrity in order to obtain something, usually for selfish motives)*. My self-respect is not for sale. If the customer is disrespecting me, my product or company, I won't tolerate it just to make a sale. When I was younger and much less experienced, I was a "nice guy." In many situations this nice-guy *"unwillingness to stand up for himself"* demeanor came across as being weak and many people treated me accordingly. Weak people don't close many deals, other than sympathy sales. Stand up for yourself when someone is acting inappropriately. There will always be more potential customers to sell to. In fact, many strong people will respect you more if you are willing to stand up for yourself, *even* if it costs you a sale. Often customers are just testing you. You have to live with yourself for a long time. Money comes and goes, but self-respect lasts a lifetime. Always give your customers your best performance and they will usually respond in kind. Whoever is asking the questions is the one who is in control. You must lead the sales presentation no matter whether on the phone or in person. Learn how to do this without becoming obnoxious – it is possible.

During your performance, your duty is to educate your customer on why doing business with you is a win for them which they simply cannot do without. Always be on their side. You are THEIR advocate first, and the company's second. Do right by the customer and your company will still love you because you will be bringing in the most deals. It is all about results. Performance is all that matters. I should not have to state this by now, but I will anyway. Do not ever mislead or lie to your customer, no matter who they are (spouse, child, business customer, etc.). Only make promises that you can deliver. A customer can and will accept some product shortfalls when they like the person they are buying from. However, a customer seldom forgives someone when they believe that person misled them just to get their money.

Study, learn, listen, understand, ask a lot of questions, and do whatever is necessary to honestly build the NEED and create a win-win. Worry more about giving the customer what they need than about whatever you want to get from the sale (money, incentive, recognition, etc.), and you won't have to worry about yourself. Your team should take good care of you because ultimately *you* are their customer, aren't you? Perform like a rock star and everything else can be worked out.

9.5.4 Close

In every sales presentation there is a sale made. Either the customer buys what you are selling, and everybody wins, or you buy the excuse they are selling to justify their not buying, and everybody loses. Your choice!

<u>Lesson # 1</u>. *Offend?* Closing the sale is filling the NEED you created during the performance portion of the sales process, wrapping it up with a nice string and bow. I often find new salespeople are the most afraid of the closing portion of the sales process because now they have to overcome the customer's potential objections and this may involve dealing with perceived confrontation. I had a lot of struggle with this in the beginning. Every J.O.B. I had ever had taught me how to be a servant (factory, nurse's aide, busboy and waiter), so to stand up and direct the sales process and be tough during the close was very difficult for me. I was also raised to not offend people. In order to succeed at anything in life, not just sales, you must stop being a "nice guy" who accepts other people's excuses or a "people-pleaser" who will do anything in order to keep the peace. No longer can you afford to be afraid to offend or challenge others. Believe in what you do and what you sell and don't give up. Stand up for what you believe in, stay strong, and stick to the fight until you and the customer win.

<u>Lesson # 2</u>. *Stick with it.* There are different schools of thought on this one. Some sources say you should prepare for at least five objections and others say nine. The specific number does not matter as much as your preparation to overcome the five to nine most common objections your customer will give you. Anticipate the objection and strive to overcome it within the **Perform** portion of the sales process. This way you have the potential objection out of the way long before the customer has even had the chance to raise it. This is done by asking skillful questions and making deliberate statements to get the customer in agreement with what you believe.

There is also a belief that you should <u>Always Be Closing</u> (the

ABCs of sales), but I don't buy into this line of thinking. Perform when you are supposed to in order to properly set up the close. This aggressive-approach belief is on one side of the sales spectrum and the more timid talking-yourself-out-of-a-sale situation is on the other. Both over-selling and not-closing-at-all end the same with NO deal, and the reasons people make these mistakes are weakness, self doubt, fear to offend, and lack of training. Basically, know when to talk and be deliberate about what you say and do in order to create the NEED and also know when to shut up. Do not allow yourself to get diarrhea of the mouth just because you are nervous.

<u>Lesson # 3.</u> *1, 2, 3 GO.* You can overcome every objection using a three-step process. Every objection is an opportunity to educate your customer again in why this is a winning proposition for them. Initially I became frustrated by objections, as if I assumed nobody would give them to me. Now I realize what the customer is really saying is, "I do not understand enough yet to justify giving you _____ for what you are selling. I need more information so I can feel good that this is a smart decision for me." Fill in the blank with words like money, time, or whatever it is you want to get from them in this sale. To overcome their objection, you must help them FEEL like this purchase makes sense and that they are making a wise choice by buying from you. When they like you, and what you are selling makes sense, they will buy!!!

1. <u>Empathy.</u> When the customer objects to your closing question, always respond with, "*I understand, but ...*" or "*I would feel the same way, but ...*" or any other statement which puts you and them empathically on the same team. I understand their position but that does not mean I agree with it or have to accept it. I show empathy and actually listen intently to what they have to say. This is a reason why I did not wear a watch while doing a sales presentation. The process is supposed to be about helping

them, so I do not care how long it takes to accomplish this task. My goal is not to just do a bunch of non-productive presentations. Who wins then? Showing empathy breaks down barriers rather than competing with the customer, which will only add to the difficulties.

2.   <u>Skillful Questions and Deliberate Statements.</u> Success is not accidental. Once you have expressed empathy, metaphorically grab the customer by the hand and lead them down the mental path you want them to go. By asking skillful questions and making deliberate statements, my ultimate purpose is to get the customer to a point of AGREEMENT. When they agree with me, I can then move on to step three and ask a *closing question* again.

When you are asking questions, you are in control of the process because it forces them to open their mind to search for an answer. **When you ask a question, wait for as long as it takes until you get an answer.** If you ask a question and because of your impatience or nervousness, proceed to answer it or go onto something else, you have said loud and clear that your original question did not matter much anyway. The main reason to get your point across in question form as much as possible is, *Telling is NOT Selling*.

Few people like to be told what to do. Most like to be respected enough to be asked what they think about something. Effective communication is about drawing the customer closer to you and breaking down barriers to developing the relationship. Telling them what to do or think does not go very far toward bringing the customer and you closer together. I understand you cannot get every key point across in the form of a question; sometimes you have to make statements. However, I still use questions to lead into making statements. Remember the ultimate purpose of step two is to get them to a point of obvious agreement with your position, as if they would be foolish not to agree with you.

My final point and certainly one of the most important to properly asking questions is to NEVER ask *Yes* or *No* questions, unless you absolutely positively know what the answer will be before asking the question. For example, if you ask someone, "Would you like me to slap your face?" unless they are rather strange, obviously the answer would be a clear *"NO!"* This is a fair assumption to make and asking obvious questions has its purpose, too. You are leading your customer down the mental path to agreement and cannot allow a fork in the road to develop. Instead of asking, *"Would you like me to do a presentation for you?"* Ask, *"Would tomorrow at ___ or ___ be better?"* Give them a choice between Yes and Yes. This is really Sales 101 material but nonetheless extremely important. Strategic questions combined with skillful statements lead to superior results.

3.   <u>Ask the closing question.</u> When a closing question is asked and answered, the deal is done. When you say to the customer, *"Would you prefer to use cash, check, or charge for this today?"* and they respond with, *"Check,"* the deal is done, sealed, over, sayonara! So SHUT UP, fill out the order, take your stuff and go home to celebrate. First empathize, next get the customer to a point of obvious agreement, and then get an answer to your buying question. Now it is time to wrap everything up as quickly as possible and leave, so there is not any chance of talking yourself out of the deal.

This exact strategy can be used for any type of sale you want to close. Again let us use the example of asking someone out on a date. Empathy – *"I understand but I am really not that bad-looking."* Agreement – *"Wouldn't you agree that you have been on a date with worse at least once?"* Answer – Yes. Closing Question – *"So would you rather I pick you up tomorrow at 7 or 8 p.m.?"* Answer – 8. Smile, shut up, and leave!

This three-step process to overcome any objection is simple but effective. You can use it for every single objection you will face in life. Remember to stay on task. Do not talk too much. Be deliberate and focused and you will close the deal.

The most common objections I have seen, which apply to almost every method of sales and type of product, are:

- It is too expensive.
- I want to think it over.
- I am just looking.
- I want delivery by this date or else.
- I am not interested.
- I need to talk it over with _____.
- I am not sure why I should buy from you.

Anticipate and prepare for these and any other common objections to your method or product type. Anticipation, preparation, and practice are the keys to overcoming any and all objections you will receive. Don't sweat anything that comes up. Roll with it all. Even if you make a mistake on one presentation, the next customer won't know it. Each presentation is an opportunity to get stronger, better, and further along on your lifestyle journey. At my level of sales maturity, I actually enjoy getting the guy who gives me objection after objection after objection until he is blue in the face. I do my best to remain emotionally neutral and keep my cool as I press on, because one thing I know is that I will outlast him. My point is the toughest customers are many times the best because it is during these presentations when you grow the most. You have no other option, correct?

Lesson # 4. *Assume the sale.* Throughout the presentation you are not hoping or wanting this deal – you expect and NEED it. You assume the positive. You have a very good idea of what they NEED in most cases, before you even communicate with them because of your skillful BEFORE due diligence work.

You don't say, *"If they buy ..."* Instead you say, *"When they buy..."* By assuming the positive you make winning a foregone conclusion before you even walk into the arena for battle. An example of this would be to have an Order Form sitting out for everyone to clearly see, but have it off to the side. It should already be filled out with the customer's basic information (name, address, phone, etc.) because you did this BEFORE in preparation for the win. The customer will typically think you are very confident in your company, product, and yourself to have taken this step, therefore they are more likely to be confident as well because they like and believe in you.

9.5.5 After

After the sale is done IS your greatest opportunity to truly shine. Unfortunately, in many instances, the moment someone gets the money they think the sale is over. They could not be more wrong. This is their poor attitude, poor training, immaturity, lack of experience, and selfishness showing brightly. Instead, the dance with your customer has only just begun. Develop a reputation as someone who not only delivers what they promised but, whenever possible, do more. Doing more will always come back to you.

I sent thank-you cards to my personal safety equipment customers once a year for the three years following the actual sale. Why? First to thank them for their initial order; later, I just wanted to keep my name in front of them when they needed something more, or knew of someone who did. Keeping yourself in front of the customer is especially important when you sell a consumable product or service. It costs far less per sale to resell an existing customer than it does to bring in a new one, and successful people are constantly focused upon productivity. A simple "thank you" shows appreciation, humility, and just the kind of person you are. They feel even better for having done business with YOU and you have just validated their affinity for you. It also proves you are committed to furthering the relationship by keeping it alive, after all business is just relationship development. This will pay dividends for years to come. I can do business with anybody I want to but **choose** to go back again and again to the few people who made me **feel appreciated**.

Do whatever fits into your industry and budget to stay in contact with and show appreciation for your customer. When they need your product and/or service again, they will call you because you are their friend who stays in touch. Why would they ever go anywhere else?

Also in the AFTER part of the sales process, spend time reflecting upon what went well and/or poorly during the entire procedure. Ask yourself skillful questions to study why someone did or did not purchase and determine what you can do better next time. This simple evaluation will ensure you do not make the same mistakes again and again and again, which always leads to greater productivity. Analyze and study every element of your process looking for opportunities to improve. Then document what you determined to work or not work for future reference for yourself or for others when you are in a leadership role. Good record-keeping will make your team far more productive because they will not have to waste nearly as much time making the same mistakes you did. Instead they can just be productive and profitable for themselves and the team. An in-depth understanding of both your successes and setbacks will better prepare you to lead, and that is where the big money is earned.

It doesn't matter if you want to actually work as a sales person, a cosmetologist, or manager at a grocery store because these sales lessons and information are universal. Once again, sales is just effective communication to create win-win situations. And being a great communicator will help you be the most productive you can be at whatever you choose as your lifestyle vehicle. What is in this book will allow everyone who reads and applies the information to become better communicators, thereby helping our entire community by being better spouses, parents, civic leaders, business people, and individuals.

By learning to fish, you will indeed set yourself free to enjoy your dream lifestyle, instead of just continuing to exist only to earn a living!

9.6 Truth # 9 Action Points

The game of money is an eye-opener when you look at it honestly. How much longer are you going to continue to be merely a pawn being played with, while working hard to support the government and make other people rich? Your typical way of life is your choice. Is the life of the average American right for you? If not, then stop remaining dependent by taking the fish from *The Man* and instead learn how to be independent and free by catching them on your own?

A.   <u>Decide you will no longer accept the tainted fish.</u> Both the government and your current employer have a vested interest in keeping you as one of the numb sheeple stuck in the daily grind. You could continue that way or study the rules of this game of money in order to live like the rich do and pay only what is legally required. However, you cannot be an owner of your own productivity until you stop accepting and eating the tainted J.O.B. fish.

B.   <u>Learn how to fish on your own with a single fishing pole, then a net.</u> It starts with your decision to pick a different financial vehicle to drive during your lifestyle journey. In order to get the most out of it, you next must learn how this new vehicle functions at its peak level of productivity. Get together with the best driving instructor you can find, and learn exactly how to get the greatest performance out of this engine. Gradually seek to become a driving instructor yourself in order to help others and in turn, earn the serious money. Once in a sales position, you can fish for your own dinner with a single fishing pole. Once into leadership, you begin to use a net and make money 24/7/365.

C.   <u>Learn, understand, and use the Sales Process to climb your Victory Mountain.</u> THINK like a successful person does and you attract success. Once your mind is ready to produce, be sure you have the right environment in order to get the best results. Prepare BEFORE to win. Pick your method, product, and team based upon what gets you excited. Excited people produce. Hire slowly and fire fast. PERFORM like a rock star to create the *need* and then fill the *need* you created – CLOSE the deal. Finally become a master of the AFTER to insure continued success. This is how you consistently reach the summit of your own personal Victory Mountain. Now everyone will see the flags you have planted at the top!

STEP 3
Where are you GOING?
Summation of Action Points

Truth # 7
Success in life is a journey,
NOT a destination

A. Choose your path.
B. Stay between the lines.
C. Seek life fulfillment.

Truth # 8
Never ever quit!

A. Overcome fear.
B. Remain persistent.
C. Develop your self-discipline.

Truth # 9:
Learning to fish will set you free!

A. Decide you will no longer accept the tainted fish.
B. Learn how to fish on your own with a single fishing pole, then a net.
C. Learn, understand, and use the Sales Process to climb your Victory Mountain.

Bonus

Financial Intelligence...

The True Path of the Rich

Instead of being cliché by seeking to become financially independent, I strove for Financial Intelligence. When I understood that money was just a way to keep score in a big game of debt and control, I decided to learn the rules of that game so I could play to win. Financially Ignorant is how I started out – I just did not know much of anything. Financially Stupid is how I was from time to time – I often knew better but still made foolish choices most often due to momentary lack of emotional discipline. Because of my decision long ago to become Financially Intelligent and Emotionally Disciplined, I gradually began to win at the money game enough to live the lifestyle I chose rather than continue to settle for what I could afford.

Again, I would much rather cry in a Rolls Royce than laugh on a bicycle, because even though money is only one of the tools necessary for lifestyle fulfillment, it is very important. Poverty is an ugly beast that helps no one. Having the financial depth necessary to live as you choose is important, but how do you do it? These are the action steps I followed in order to become Financially Intelligent and build my resources from nothing to the level I desired. Learn and implement them in an emotionally disciplined manner and you, too, can make the journey to whatever level of financial success you desire.

1 Decide to DEDFIL. Money is a result of actions taken and my actions focused upon Developing my *Emotional Discipline* – so I would keep the money once I generated it, *Financial Intelligence* – so I would know how to create the money from nothing, and *Leadership* – because in order to live the lifestyle I decided was right for me, I would need a lot of money, so I had to be able to lead an entire fleet of fishermen. I believed that by becoming more and more Financially Intelligent, I would then make smarter decisions and as a result eventually become financially independent. This commitment to constantly learn more about money and how to best use it is never ending.

2 Define Success. I created my own personal definition of financial independence, so I had a clear target to drive toward deliberately. I refused to wander from point to point HOPING to stumble onto economic freedom. My definition of being financially free is when my investments, without needing much or any personal involvement, generate enough income to cover my current expenses. I also understood that getting rich, just like being poor, does NOT happen overnight. This understanding helped me to

avoid **some** but not all of the *get rich quick* pitfalls, learn more from the ones I got caught in, and not become overly discouraged during the tough times.

3   Mental Development. I had to recondition my mind to eliminate any existing negative references to being financially successful and other limiting money beliefs. Money is merely a lifestyle achievement tool NOT the root of all evil. Money does not change people! Money simply is an amplifier because it provides them the ability to be more of what they already are inside. If they are good people, they will get better by being able to help more people. If they are a drunk, they will just drink a better brand. If they were financially ignorant or stupid before winning the lottery, just adding more fuel to the fire won't magically make them Financially Intelligent. Until you get educated you will remain ignorant.

4   Accountability. I struggled with, but had to get over, jealousy of other successful people. Admittedly, I have been jealous and bitter that other people seemed to have so much more than I did. During my self-pity parties I would ask myself, "Why is everything such a fight for me?" This of course never did me any good. Jealousy keeps you in a negative mindset from which personal growth is nearly impossible. And allowing myself to feel the victim of being born poor or wallow in my own self-pity was foolish at best. If I had kept that mindset, I would never have broken free from being financially destitute. I had to accept accountability and stop blaming others. I alone controlled my financial situation upon becoming an adult because now either I made it happen or allowed it to happen to me.

5 Personal Productivity Ownership. So long as you allow the government to get paid before you or allow your employer to profit more off your productivity than you, becoming Financially Independent will most likely remain a mere wish. At age 19, I traded in my last J.O.B. (a limited financial vehicle) for ownership (a much faster higher-powered vehicle). As a result of thinking like other rich people, I took ownership of my own time, emotional energy, and experience and then took deliberate action to most intelligently invest and direct my productivity to achieve the greatest results.

6 Results Pay. I accepted that ALL of my near-future income would not be guaranteed by anything except my own personal performance. If I did not produce, I did not eat – period! By not giving myself any other option other than success, I created within myself a *Sense of Urgency* that no one could take away. I decided to no longer confuse hard work with results. Just because someone works hard does not ensure they will get positive results. In order to succeed, to live the lifestyle of your dreams, winners at the game of life do whatever is necessary to get the results needed. Winners do not just work 8-hour days or 40-hour weeks. Winners don't whine about the labor pains of life, they just show everyone the baby!

7 Overcome Fear. I realized I could not travel to my desired destination without first leaving my starting point. To avoid rusting where it sits, every ship must lift its anchor and eventually leave the safety of its harbor in order to make its voyage. At the beginning of every new voyage I am scared, but leave myself no choice but to face my fears. As a result of Mental Momentum, over time, fear's grip lessens but never completely goes away. Small, gradual, deliberate steps taken in the right direction, outside of one's comfort zone, over a long period of time, are what build the confidence necessary to keep fear at bay. Clarity of destination is crucial to being willing to take action and the ability to make proper course corrections along the way – decisions based upon accurate information instead of fear.

8 Examples to Follow. I found the owner's manual for my financial vehicle by seeking real-life "how to" information from others who had walked the path from rags to riches, and I could then model my life around what actually worked. I obtained this Financial Intelligence information by asking real people face-to-face, used the library to source great books and tapes, and eventually developed my own library of successful experiences to draw upon as I earned more and more money. I believe there is always someone who is more successful than me, so I am committed to never stop searching for and learning from other more successful people. Because of my ever-expanding lifestyle vision and commitment to developing my Financial Intelligence, I will always remain the green piece of fruit growing on the tree. I cannot afford to allow myself to ripen and fall to the ground and begin to rot. I have too much yet to do.

9 Total Engagement. Developing my Financial Intelligence was extremely challenging because I had to first eliminate the many existing distractions in my life, whether actual or perceived, so I could completely focus upon my objective. I quit college, terminated relationships with destructive people, got rid of my J.O.B., and put myself in the right mental and physical environment to provide the greatest likelihood for success. By being engaged fully in my lifestyle journey, I became a man on a mission and would not allow anyone or anything to get in my way. I was willing to go it alone for as long as necessary because I believed my vehicle would eventually pick up speed and then plenty of other good people would want to join me since everyone wants to be a part of a winning team.

10 Open Mind and Eyes. I constantly keep my mind open to recognize new opportunities for growth and investment. I am willing to take risks and get back up after being knocked down. I stopped talking about it and took action to pay my dues. I never looked for the free lunch for fear a string would be attached. I understood that not all ventures would work out and I might get taken advantage of a few times until I learned better. I went into all opportunities striving to keep my eyes open in order to be as realistic and emotionally-neutral as possible, all the while staying positive and expecting everything to work out well. During the toughest of times, in order to keep myself driving forward, I relied heavily upon my absolute decision to live free, which required a certain level of income. Quitting or settling were never options.

11 Team Building. I kept my ideal lifestyle always in mind as I built my Emotional Support, Peak Performance, and Task-Doer Teams. Success is a team sport and in order to achieve what I needed, I had to enlist the help of other key people. I only allowed beneficial people to join my teams and quickly eliminated those who were not – hire slowly and fire fast. I knew a high level of personal productivity would be necessary to succeed, therefore

I could not afford to keep any emotional or financial leeches. Again, I was willing to go it alone until I found the right people who were willing and excited to participate in the journey on my terms. Good team members ADD more than they cost.

12   <u>Personal Success Routine and Coach</u>. I hired multiple coaches until I gradually found those great ones who helped me to develop my Success Routine. As a result of my routine, I knew what I had to do at all times in order to get the biggest returns on my mental and physical investments. At the risk of being overly redundant, I say again, success is not accidental – the person on top of the mountain did not fall there. In addition to my routine, I needed someone to help keep me on track and hold me accountable for results. Also, I needed the same person to help get me back in line when my vehicle started to drift onto the shoulder. When you attempt to go it alone, often you won't even be aware you are off track until your vehicle drives off of a financial cliff and it's too late. If you survive, you may need to begin your journey all over again with a whole new vehicle. My best coaches have been worth every penny I paid them and more because they gradually helped me transition my Financial Intelligence into Financial Wisdom. Find the best coach you can and enlist their help to develop your own success routine which will bring out the best in you again and again.

13   <u>Cut the Chains.</u> As long as you allow yourself to remain a slave to bad-debt, you will only be making other people rich. By lacking the Emotional Discipline and Financial Intelligence to resist the temptation of immediate gratification, you will stay a broke resident of Regretsville but have many shiny

beads, trinkets, and regrets to keep you company. To become and remain bad-debt free, I kept a tight accounting of every penny because I had zero money to waste. I had to understand where my money was flowing in order to direct it properly. In order to track spending effectively, I stopped using cash and only used checks and credit cards because both of them leave a paper trail to follow and of course all credit cards were paid off monthly. In addition, I had a stranglehold on my financial situation by gaining a complete understanding of my own income statement and balance sheet. My clear picture of where I was on my journey at all times enabled me to spot holes from which money was leaking so I could plug them, and maximize payment of debt until I was free of the chains.

14

Invest In Yourself. As I paid off debt, I lived modestly, which allowed me to spend all of my extra money where I could get the most out of each dollar. I started by investing in my single greatest asset – myself. I spent lots of money on mental-development materials which focused on self-improvement, sales, management, leadership, and financial planning. I also paid for personal training at the gym, seminars of all varieties, and joined numerous successful groups so I could learn what they knew that I didn't. By developing myself first, I became more valuable to those I led, which caused them to believe in me and as a result produce even more. As a result of building people, my income increased exponentially. My success has always been rooted in personal development first and then an increase in life's bounty will follow as a result.

15 <u>Safety Net & Income Producing Investments.</u> Once debt-free I began to direct my money into investments to strengthen and amplify my financial future, such as a 12-month emergency fund, paper investments (stocks, bonds, etc.), and other businesses and real estate. My asset purchases, and those of the other successful people I have known, are done with specific intentions of building a portfolio of investments to either fund my desired lifestyle or sell in order to raise even more money to invest. I am very aware of how much money I need in order to continue funding my current and future desired lifestyle. Because of knowing exactly what I was aiming to hit, strategically seeking out and acquiring the necessary income producing investments became only a matter of time, education, and work rather than a mystery to fear.

16 <u>Invest in Others.</u> I reinvest a constant flow of money into development of new training materials like this book for my customers. The people who work with my businesses are part of our team and those team members are my primary customers. If my customer does not succeed, neither do I. In addition to developing myself, I believe my customers could be even more productive, so I have invested in providing them with the best tools available. As a result, they are better able to develop themselves, which in turn creates more income for everyone and we all win as a team in the long run. I do not believe controlling or limiting people is the best way to achieve genuine financial prosperity. I have to feel good about what I do, so my focus is to build people and those people will build the business. The smartest and most self-aware team members will realize they are growing and remain extremely loyal and stay with our team for a very long time through thick and thin. Investing in other good people will pay significant long-term dividends. Accept that mistakes will be made. Not everyone will be as honorable as you and me, but we must not allow the fear of poor-quality people to stop us from enriching other people's lives.

17 Record Keeping. I wrote in my journals and kept extremely accurate financial records. I often audio and video recorded meetings and because of recording what I did right, wrong, and how I felt about it, I have numerous extremely valuable life-experience reference tools. I have these for my own personal use and share them with anyone else I choose. To make the journey yourself is great, but to be able to provide others with an accurate, successful road map is even better.

18 Karma. Everything I do is based upon the belief that we will get back what we give out. I believe karma is real because we do not exist in a vacuum and what we do has an effect upon others. We cannot just take without giving. Because of this belief I volunteer my time, donate to multiple charities, motivationally speak to school children, and do my best to answer the call to help whenever it comes in. My early decision to be an example to follow has helped me continue to desire to help others who seek to help themselves no matter the obstacles life put in my path.

I will always believe ultimately the level of joy we experience in our lives is dependent upon the amount of other people we help enjoy their lives as well. What we give out comes back to us 10-fold – bad & good!

Epilogue

Our Vision Quest has begun ...

Help Wanted

**$100,000+ income opportunity
No experience necessary!**

Rapidly expanding safety equipment company filling 100 leadership positions. We are offering you a demanding personal growth adventure that requires long hours and total commitment. Only serious applicants need apply!!!

I am convinced that everyone is searching for a proven path to a better, more fulfilling life. Our quality of life is determined by our ability to think and communicate. In the end, life's winners are the clear-thinking leaders who communicate masterfully. These leaders first conceive, then sell powerful messages of hope. They focus the team upon what is possible, thereby attracting other winners to join and remain a part of the team they lead.

My passion for writing this book came from my desire to clearly communicate our team's long-range vision and concentrate our daily efforts on accomplishing Steps 1 and 2.

Step 1

Develop 100 case studies of people who earned at least $8,333 in a month after applying the information learned from this book – *100 Earning $100,000*™ (www.100E100.com).

Step 2

Analyze the case studies to create educational tools and accountability systems to market to the world.

Step 3

Generate $100,000,000 in gross sales of our coaching products which help those willing to do whatever is necessary to enjoy the lifestyles of their dreams.

In order to achieve our vision quest, we have already begun creating just the right environment in cities across America. This atmosphere is critical to properly attract, keep and develop the right people into the future leaders our movement needs. The three key environment qualities I have learned people need most to promote their advancement are detailed below.

1. **Personal growth which makes people feel significant**

   A. <u>Recognition</u> of accomplishment / proof of achievement.

   B. A sense of <u>self-worth</u> from ownership.

   C. Enough <u>confidence</u> to stand up to negative and/or destructive people.

2. **Belonging to a team which makes people feel strong**

   A. People want to be part of a team that gives them a sense of family – <u>support</u>.

   B. People need others from whom to learn and acquire <u>knowledge</u>.

   C. People need a team that provides opportunities to prove how well they are performing – <u>competition</u>.

   D. People need to belong to something that makes them feel better about who they are – <u>pride</u>.

3. **Earning enough money to make people feel successful**

   A. To feel good on a very basic level, a person must be able to earn enough money to pay their <u>current bills.</u>

B. Once their basic financial needs are met, people want to create a sense of stability and this is met by preparing financially for a <u>stable future</u>.

C. People need money to pay their bills, set aside enough to insure a stable future AND then be able to live their day-to-day lives as they choose – enough money to pay for their <u>IDEAL lifestyle</u>.

I have firmly staked our vision flag for the whole world to see. Now our team must make the journey as the world watches and judges. When you are a part of a winning team that stays focused and strong, everything is possible! Offering people an opportunity to get off their knees and become Desheepitized has been the greatest, most satisfying part of my life.

I am blessed and thankful for having been given the opportunity to write this book and lead our team to help people live as they desire. This process has been an amazingly humbling journey of introspection and understanding for me.

Now it is your time to get started.

May your travels be filled with laughter, love, and lots of FUN!

Living Deliberately "100E100"

Mr. Allen Kronebusch

Glossary

100E100

A shortened version of Step 1 of *The $100,000,000 March™* which means within AKE we will help 100 people earn incomes exceeding $100,000 per year (100 Earning $100,000).

Action Steps

Part of the Success Formula. These steps are what specifically must be done each day in order to achieve the Progress (results) necessary and accomplish the goal by the agreed upon deadline. Determine the goal first, then break it into daily Progress Steps, and finally determine the Action Steps.

Anti-Sheepitization™

This is the essence of the our team's purpose. To provide people with the tools necessary to break free and stop remaining part of the herd as a "sheeple." This is both a way of rebellious thinking and a way of living that passionately embraces being and remaining free to choose our own lifestyle.

Business

Building win-win relationships using effective people-relations.

Code of Honor

A person's promise to themselves and internal compass which points them in the right direction and helps them resist destructive temptations.

Confidence

See Mental Momentum.

DEDFIL™
Our team's motto of Developing Emotionally Disciplined, Financially Intelligent Leaders.

Desheepitized
The process of evolving from being a "sheeple" to an independent-minded person willing to do whatever is necessary to live life as they choose.

Emotional Support Team (EST)
These are the people you allow closest to you. They emotionally support you and add to your emotional energy. They challenge you and show you empathy instead of sympathy.

Emotional Discipline
The ability to control your own emotions so you are able to make better decisions (a.k.a. Emotional Neutrality).

Empathy
The process of understanding the other person's situation, listening openly without getting sucked in, and offering realistic experience-based solutions to solve the challenge and help the person.

Evaluation Points
Pause points within the Success Formula used to study and evaluate progress, either good or bad. As a result of the evaluation, action may be taken to alter the plan in order to insure successful completion of the goal by the deadline.

Financial Intelligence
The lifelong pursuit of better understanding how the game of money is really played as well as how to create money from whence there was nothing.

Financially Free
When someone's investments, without needing much or any personal involvement by them, generate enough income to cover their current expenses.

Financial Wisdom
Instead of only drawing upon one's own financial experience, learn from the wisdom of other successful people in order to make even smarter money decisions avoiding many costly mistakes.

Goal Performance Chart (GPC)
The two-part chart used to plan, record, track, and evaluate Action and Progress Steps performed. Part one is a simple recording of numeric data and part two is turning that data into an easy-to-understand image to be used during the next Evaluation Point.

J.O.B.
Acronym for Just Over Broke. This is how many people feel as they work their jobs. Their employer pays them just enough so they don't quit and often they work just hard enough so they don't get fired.

Leadership
Effectively communicating (selling) your ideas in a manner resulting in other people taking the desired action, which helps both the team and individual to win.

Life Fulfillment Formula
See Success Formula.

Life Fulfillment Team
See Success Team.

Life GPA
This is your ability to consistently achieve what you desire.

Lifestyle
A person's way of life, which is the result of their decisions made – good or bad.

Lifestyle Triangle
See Tres Elements.

Mental Momentum
The feeling of knowing you will win simply because you have entered the race. This starts out slowly at first but gradually gains speed exponentially as you win again and again. The more you achieve, the more your confidence will grow.

Path of Excuses
This path leads to Regretsville. It is filled with the never-ending pain of regrets resulting from unfulfilled hopes, dreams, and wasted lives. People who travel this path blame others for their misfortune and continue to make new excuses to justify their lack of success and happiness in life.

Path of Performance
This path in life is the only truly rewarding one. It is a path filled with strife and pain but here the pain is only momentary. This is the path of a warrior.

Peak Performance Team (PPT)
You ask these people to join your team because they have a specific skill to offer. They are paid to teach you and challenge your way of thinking. Because of what they do and know, you will perform at peak efficiency.

People Studies
The process of understanding why people do what they do when they do it, and the art of applying this understanding to affect other people's behavior.

Personal Financial Statement
A picture of how your own income statement and balance sheet relate. This shows how your money flows in and out, along with a detailed comparison between your assets and debts.

Personal Inventory
See Personal Financial Statement.

Personal Productivity
The sum total of a person's time + emotional energy + experience. This is how an employer gets rich by purchasing cheaply from their employees.

Plan
A person's daily routine which consists of their Action and Progress steps developed with careful thought in order to achieve a goal by a specific deadline (a.k.a. Success Routine).

Planning Calendar (PC)
Used along with a Goal Performance Chart to assist in creation of and successful implementation of a person's goal-achievement plan.

Progress Steps
Part of the Success Formula. After breaking down a goal, these are the bite-size pieces that must be done every day in order to achieve the goal by the agreed-upon deadline. First the goal, then Progress Steps, and finally Action Steps.

Reward Points
Pause points within the Success Formula when someone rewards themselves for positive results obtained. As a result of this regular reward strategy, the person striving for the goal is more likely to continue because they feel good, and complete their goal by the deadline.

Sales

The art of using effective communication to transfer one person's belief to another.

Sales Process

Illustrated by the Victory Mountain image, this is the process of closing a sale for any product, service, or idea (Think, Before, Perform, Close, After).

Sheeple

A derogatory term to describe those who have given up on their dreams. They have accepted their place in the herd and no longer fight to make their ideal lifestyle real. Sheeple travel the Path of Excuses and live in Regretsville.

Success Score

See Life GPA.

Success Formula

The process of achieving anything in life = decision + visualize + goal + plan + action + tracking + evaluation + change + rewarding + recording.

Success Team

Someone's entire group of people helping them achieve in life. This team consists of a person's Emotional Support Team, Peak Performance Team, and Task-Doer Team.

Sympathy

The process of sharing in another person's pain and/or negative situation often used as a tool to control. Sympathy does not fix the problem.

Task-Doer Team (TDT)

This is your service team. These people add to your quality of life by freeing up your time and emotional energy by doing the tasks you would rather not. By paying them to do everything else, these people give you the ability to specialize in doing what you are best at and most enjoy doing.

Tres Elements
The combination of Mental, Physical, and Spiritual health ultimately leading to life fulfillment.

I have read a lot of good books focused on business, self-development, and personal philosophies. But the challenge I so often have with them is they do not give you a clear place to apply what you just learned. Kind of like winding up a little toy and letting it bounce around aimlessly on a tabletop without a clear direction to channel the energy. Good books often get me wound up but provide nowhere specific to invest my energy. For this reason, I decided to make this book different.

Recommended Reading:

Managing by Harold Geneen

Rich Dad Poor Dad by Robert T. Kiyosaki

The Millionaire Mind by Thomas J. Stanley

Made in America by Sam Walton and John Huey

Now Discover Your Strengths by Marcus Buckingham and Donald O. Clifton

The E-Myth by Michael E. Gerber

Good to Great by Jim Collins